Writing
Your Life Story

Writing
Your Life Story

How to record and present your memories for friends and family to enjoy

Michael Oke

howtobooks

Published by How To Books Ltd,
3 Newtec Place, Magdalen Road,
Oxford OX4 1RE, United Kingdom.
Tel: (01865) 793806. Fax: (01865) 248780.
info@howtobooks.co.uk
www.howtobooks.co.uk

First edition 2001
Reprinted 2002

British Library Cataloguing in Publication Data.
A catalogue record for this book is available from
the British Library.

Cover design by Baseline Arts Ltd, Oxford
Cartoons by Mike Flanagan

Produced for How To Books by Deer Park Productions
Typeset by Anneset, Weston-super-Mare, N Somerset
Printed and bound by Cromwell Press, Trowbridge, Wiltshire

NOTE: The material contained in this book is set out in good
faith for general guidance and no liability can be accepted
for loss or expense incurred as a result of relying in particular
circumstances on statements made in the book. Laws and
regulations are complex and liable to change, and readers should
check the current position with the relevant authorities before
making personal arrangements.

Contents

Foreword

Long ago I had a Granny and a Grandma. They were both white-haired gentle women.

Granny, the Scottish one, liked to read Westerns as she rocked in her chair and sucked on a toffee. Grandma once ran a stall at Newbiggin beach in the North-East, and chaired meetings using an olivewood gavel.

I'd like to tell you more, but I know hardly anything else about them. I will never know what songs they sang as they washed up, which flowers they loved, or what views they held.

When they died, effectively, for me, they disappeared without trace. There were old photographs but in this context they are hardly worth a thousand words.

If only they had left a written account of their lives . . .

I believe that one of the greatest gifts we can give to our families, and bequeath to those who follow us, is an intimate, first-hand account of our lives. Thousands of *Yours* readers have done just that.

This book will make the task of capturing you and your life enjoyable for you, and enriching for those who read it. Mike Oke feels passionately that everyone has within them a marvellous story – the tale of their life. He's just the man to help you tell it.

Neil Patrick
Editor-in-Chief
Yours *magazine*

Acknowledgements

I have had the privilege of helping dozens of people to write their life stories – the enjoyment that this has given me is immense. All of these friends have helped me in the compilation of this book and my thanks go to them.

I would also like to thank Sally Gray of *Bound Biographies* for her support and expertise, as well as the valued advice of Sylvia Culverhouse, Malcolm Tait, Tom Rayfield and my father, Michael Oke.

Neil Patrick of *Yours* magazine has been a loyal supporter of my work for many years and I am grateful for his kind words in the Foreword.

A special tribute is due to my wife Mychelle for her unceasing support, encouragement and love – thank you.

My final thanks are again extended to the many wonderful friends who have allowed me to assist them with their life stories, and especially to the memory of Roy Barton with whom it all began.

Michael Oke

Introduction

Everyone is special and everyone has a book inside them.

The main premise of this book is to inspire, cajole and provide practical advice for anyone who has had thoughts of committing their memories to paper. Help is also offered in the presentation of the manuscript to produce a few books for friends and family.

This book is primarily intended for the enthusiastic hobbyist . . . although those with greater ambition will also find it of value.

You may not have written the first word of your life story, or perhaps you have started but become bogged down, lost enthusiasm or just thought, 'What's the point – who's going to read it?' You may even have written the manuscript and now want to tidy it up and present it in book form. Whatever your situation, this book is for you.

Of course, you may want your parents to write, or perhaps you would like to assist them . . . help will also be given in this.

Please don't feel daunted at the thought of writing a book – simply write the way you speak and you are half-way there already. People love you for who you are – sharing that with them in print will be all the more of a celebration.

Taken a step at a time, maybe writing just a few episodes of your life, you will see that it is not as daunting as it first appears . . . and also what fun it can be.

This book is not a heavy tome, and you certainly do not have to be a literary giant to write your life story. If you can write a letter, you really can write a book. You need have had no writing experience at all. Writing is simply speaking on paper.

Some define a successful autobiography as one that makes it onto the bookshelves of *W.H. Smith*. My definition, on the other hand, is a book which truly reflects and celebrates the life of the person concerned; one where the reader gets to know the writer, and when in years to come the book is read by people not yet born, they too will get a flavour of the author.

This guide is intended to be practical and fun. Writing your life story is a project which will be with you for many months – it is my intention to make it as enjoyable a hobby as possible.

You might want to record some of the incredible social and technological changes you have witnessed in your life. Perhaps you remember the war, evacuation, rationing, your first black and white television set, man on the moon . . . after all, the past fifty or so years have seen more change than any other period in history. During the early part of the twentieth century Granny was invariably to be seen all in black, and wearing long skirts – today she is just as likely to be wearing leggings at an aerobics class!

In addition to copious memory joggers, ideas are provided regarding what to include and perhaps what to omit. Suggestions are also made for dealing with the more difficult moments. Throughout all this, please remember that there is no right or wrong way to write your life story. after all, it is *your* life story.

Advice is also provided regarding how to transform your manuscript into a book . . . if that is what you want. There is nothing wrong with a photocopied handwritten manuscript presented in a ring binder. While the story is the most important part, for those seeking a more professional presentation, technology is available for books to be produced in low numbers and to a small budget. Pictures – black and white, sepia and colour – can be reproduced to an excellent standard, and single volumes can be presented in impressive leather bindings.

You may want to read the book from cover to cover, or prefer to pick and choose the chapters you require. Decide what suits you best but, most of all, enjoy the process of writing your life story.

Ultimately, the intention of this book is to help you celebrate your life and those who have been special to you. So, whether you want to write for yourself or because someone is bullying you, have a go, you'll be glad you did.

You are special and your life is special . . . share it.

Michael Oke

1

Reasons for Writing Your Life Story

Knowing why you want to write your life story will influence what is included. This chapter will look at reasons for writing, as well as, hopefully, providing inspiration for those not yet convinced of the validity of such a project.

KNOWING WHY YOU WANT TO WRITE

There are many reasons to write and it is likely that at least one of the following will strike a chord.

Nursing a desire to write

Maybe you have never had the time, or possibly the confidence, to start writing until now. Alternatively, you may have kept a diary all your life and now want it collated and edited into a book. This is your opportunity.

Remembering parents or grandparents

How many times do we look at boxes of old photographs and wish we knew something about the faces before us? There may not even be any names on the back to identify the people.

As time passes so there are fewer people who have memories of those from a previous generation. You might be the only person who still remembers your grandparents. If you do not record what you know of their lives these precious details will be lost forever.

Interestingly, as you write about your parents and grandparents, you may well spot patterns which you and perhaps your children have repeated.

Responding to a request to write

This might be by a family member, perhaps a child, grandchild, nephew or niece, or maybe a friend has been nagging at you to put pen to paper.

It is now part of the National Curriculum to seek 'eyewitness accounts', so perhaps a neighbour's child has sown the seed for this autobiographical adventure.

Biographies are the most popular form of reading . . . they are even more interesting when they are about someone you know.

CASE STUDY – Celebrating Sid's life

Sid and Mary decided to write a joint book. They felt it best not to confer, and while they knew that they would undoubtedly cover some of the same material, it would be interesting to read of events from a different viewpoint.

Sid had just written about their wedding day when he became ill. Sadly, Sid deteriorated rapidly and died within six weeks.

It was several months before Mary was able to contemplate writing again. Many tears were shed as she read what Sid had written, but she felt resolved to continue – she even decided to include a few of the many tributes received from friends when Sid died.

The project became a celebration of Sid and Mary's life together, and it was a great source of comfort for Mary to know that Sid would live on through the book. The final volume was presented to the family on what would have been Sid's 80th birthday.

Remembering your spouse or loved one

Writing about a lost partner or loved one can be a cathartic experience, although sometimes a period of time has to elapse before you feel ready to embark on such a project. What you write can be a wonderful tribute to a person very dear to your heart.

Providing a record for future generations of the family

Maybe the initiative has come from within to leave something for your grandchildren, your godchildren or future generations, possibly even as a surprise gift. Perhaps you wish that you had been left such a record by your forebears.

The world has changed phenomenally over the past few decades. Even a 40-year-old will remember a time before decimalisation, the unification of Germany, England winning the World Cup, using slide rules and receiving free school milk. Then there's the first time you tasted foreign food or perhaps the luxury of going abroad on holiday. All these memories and many more will provide a fascinating record of the twentieth century for future generations.

Recording a particular period of your life

You may have served in a war in some capacity, either seeing action or supporting the war effort indirectly. There again, you may have been evacuated or remember the hardships of rationing.

Alternatively, you may have had a particularly interesting childhood being brought up abroad. Perhaps you had an extended stay in hospital, or nursed a loved one through a lengthy illness at home. Such subjects make for fascinating reading, and, who knows, once you've caught the writing bug you may want to record other parts of your life.

Being inspired by a TV programme

Watching *The 1940s House* may have set you thinking about the days before electric washing machines and refrigerators. You can recall how washday was such a chore for your mother (or even yourself), and how it was doubly difficult in wet weather as the Dutch airer and clothes horse had to be used . . . no spin dryers or radiators to help in those days. Then there was Reckitt's blue, Robin starch, mangles, the copper . . .

Illustrating how the workplace has changed

Many jobs are almost unrecognisable compared with thirty or forty years ago when modern technology meant a comptometer for the book-keeper. You also probably had to clock in, losing a quarter of an hour's pay if you were so much as three minutes late.

There was an obvious hierarchy, this often being defined by the hat that was worn, be it flat cap, trilby or bowler. There was also the associated respect: the boss was 'Mr Tilbury' – no one would have called him 'Martin' . . . and, yes, the bosses were invariably men. In fact, women often had to resign when they got married!

A six-day working week was commonplace. If you were lucky perhaps you only worked Saturday mornings, leaving Saturday afternoon for shopping; there was no late night opening, and Sunday trading was inconceivable. And how many weeks holiday did you get – one or two?

Your nursing days may have been a fantastic time and you want to record how things have changed so dramatically in the medical profession. You might remember waxing the floor, or perhaps how penicillin was the wonder drug after the days of M&B 693 and 760. Perhaps you pre-date the NHS, or witnessed its infancy.

Writing a company book
You may have started a business and want to record its history, perhaps weaving chapters within your own life story. Looking at the company now, who would have believed that on one occasion you had to sell the typewriter to pay the wages?

Looking for a hobby
If you are looking for a hobby to exercise your mind, writing your life story is the perfect choice. It can be as gentle or demanding as you require, depending on whether you write purely from memory or decide to undertake more extensive research. The latter may involve visiting relatives to pick their brains, referring to some of the excellent books and videos widely available, or visiting a few of the many nostalgia museums.

Q: Don't I have to be really old before I write my life story?

A: No, just because you write your autobiography does not mean that there won't be more chapters to come. Many people write in their fifties and early sixties, some younger still.

Often the desire is sparked by a life change like retirement (or early retirement), or because the time is right to realise that ambition of writing a book. Writing about your life thus far helps to draw a line under what has gone before, allowing you to move on to your next adventure. Since completing her book, one author went trekking in China.

If you write a book in your fifties, there's nothing to stop you writing a sequel in your eighties!

Writing for yourself
Sadly, all too often people find it difficult to say, 'I am writing my life story because I want to.'

You are interesting and unique. You have insights, feelings and thoughts that you will find both stimulating and enjoyable to reflect upon and express. You will open up many wonderful memories and also be amazed at what you learn about yourself in the process.

You may have something interesting you want to say . . . or maybe it's your soapbox. Either way, you're entitled to it. Don't apologise, just enjoy the experience and celebrate your life.

Writing your autobiography is immense fun, all the more so if the process is shared – this will be considered in the next chapter.

Q: I want to write, but I have never been any good at spelling and grammar. Does it matter?

A: Please don't be deflected in your enthusiasm for writing by such fears . . . and don't use them as an excuse for not writing. The important thing is to get your story down on paper first.

     You can play around with the manuscript later if you want to – plenty of help and technology is available. Suggestions regarding consistency and editing the manuscript can be found in Chapter 11.

Receiving this book as a present

You have made a start simply by reading this far. Hopefully you will feel inspired to read on . . . and maybe even to put pen to paper.

AREAS OF CAUTION

Two further reasons for writing are considered below. However, great care must be exercised before embarking on a book with these motives in mind.

Writing to set the record straight

It might be that you have felt misunderstood, or perhaps a book has been written which tells the story differently from how you remember it. Writing to set the record straight may not necessarily be a negative focus, but if it is, great care has to be taken not to offend. The law of libel is fierce and any litigation can be financially ruinous. At best you might lose friends, at worst you might also be rendered penniless.

Think carefully before putting anything contentious into print. This book is intended for those seeking to write gentle family memoirs, not blockbusters aiming to bring down governments. If that is your intention, you should seek advice elsewhere.

Seeking fame and fortune

Unless you are one of the very few individuals who receive an advance from a publisher for a manuscript yet to be written, no guarantees can ever be made about making money from writing your memoirs. Indeed, if such an advance is forthcoming, it is likely that you are already in the 'fame and fortune' category.

Please think very carefully before you put pen to paper if your motive is financial. Apart from the well-publicised exceptions, very few 'unknown' people make money from their autobiography. Publishing is a notoriously fickle industry and this book makes no promises in the realms of publication.

Beware, there is an industry known as vanity publishing which will be discussed later. The advice here is to keep your eyes open and your chequebook closed.

As long as your reasons for writing are wholesome, you will experience a great sense of achievement and satisfaction once you have finished.

DEALING WITH MODESTY

Modesty is the biggest single reason why people do not write their life stories. We are taught to be humble and self-effacing.

Despite this, we all know someone who should write an auto-biography: the lady down the road who brought up seven children and adopted three more during the war, and the kindly octogenarian at church who has seen so much change in his lifetime. They should write their life stories . . . but me? Oh no!

Even within the family there are those we wish had written some-thing:

'Great Aunt Ethel was such a character; if only we had put the tape recorder on when she was telling us about her amazing childhood. She remembered having gas installed, and even then it was only downstairs because the pipes were charged for by the yard and her parents could not afford to have them fitted upstairs. She was given a candle when she went to bed, and so expert was her mother at cutting this to size that if Aunt Ethel was only to read for ten minutes, the candle would extinguish virtually to the second after the tenth minute had elapsed. But there are so many stories which have been forgotten.'

Q: Isn't it big-headed to write about myself?
A: If this is your concern, the odds are that you are not big-headed.
      If you were given a book written by your grandfather, you would be mesmerised from cover to cover. You certainly would not

accuse him of being big-headed; you would simply be delighted that he had left some of those cherished memories for posterity.

Just because you write your life story does not mean that you are being immodest. Indeed, if you keep it simple and write the way you speak, it will be a gentle and fascinating record for friends and family.

LISTENING TO THE EXPERTS

Set out below are some comments from those who have written their autobiographies and who have been kind enough to take the time to share what was the inspiration behind their writing:

Family life has always been very important to me. Coming from a very large and loving family has left me with many memories. A few years ago it became an obsession for me to write all these memories down for my family and future generations.

Writing my book led to many interesting events. Numerous relatives and friends have asked to read it with amazing reactions. Through this I have found out so much more about my ancestors and even met relatives I never knew existed. It has made so much difference to my life.

Mrs Brandon, Hertfordshire

We have three lovely daughters and decided to give them an early legacy of a beautiful leather-bound book of the family's memoirs. We found it great fun compiling our days of yesteryear, recalling all those little incidents, anecdotes, happy and even sad days which creep into one's lives.

We had immense pleasure in presenting our girls with a signed copy on Gordon's 70th birthday, and truly hope it will inspire them to continue with the next generation.

Mr & Mrs Boorman, Kent

My book was the compilation of diaries and photographs kept over thirty-three years when my husband and I bought a plot of land, designed and built a bungalow for ourselves.

Mrs Simpson, Gloucestershire

I had the experience of reading some of my father's war memoirs and his early life (written in an exercise book) and found it so fascinating that I felt I must pass on to my children, grandchildren and future descendants something of my life. My dad had not completed his work when he died.

Mrs Dudley, Hampshire

Jottings hoarded over many years were lying in a file intended to be rewritten sometime. All the notes were related to my years working as a nurse. Changes over the last fifty years merited record. Retirement and re-marriage meant moving house. Decision time had arrived . . . the file came too. A friend offered to help me collate the material and the book was conceived in earnest.

Mrs Mortimer, Morayshire

I wrote my story mainly for my own benefit. I had been pondering the idea for several years, as I had a lot of thoughts churning over in my head that I didn't want to talk about. One evening, late at night, I found an old exercise book and started jotting little notes down. I wrote most evenings, not because I had to, but because I really wanted to. It all seemed to flow – there was so much to write about.

Mrs Davies, Hampshire

As far back as I can remember, and that is quite some time, I always admired and can still see a photograph on my mother's lounge table of her three brothers all dressed in Scottish uniform . . . but being so young I never appreciated their loss in the Great War and Mother never mentioned their fate. I felt I must write something about what I knew of my family background to ensure that future generations were not equally in the dark.

Mr Blake, Devon

I wrote letters home during my 27 years in the Navy. When my mother died I was amazed to find them and read them avidly. I put them into a book – they make a fascinating social record.

Mr Sherwood, Kent

I kept the whole project a secret from my daughters, who were both surprised and delighted when they were presented with the book. We seldom ask our parents about their early lives, and as we become older most of us have regrets we did not do so. Hopefully I have filled in some of this information for my offspring and the grandchildren, who find life as it was for their grandmother quite unbelievable.

Mrs Long, Cheshire

CHECKLIST

- Why do you want to write your life story?

- What excites you most about the prospect of writing?

- If your grandfather had written his life story, what details would you want him to have included? Often the smallest details are the most fascinating. If my grandfather wrote that he cleaned his shoes every night, the fact that he felt it worthy of inclusion is good enough for me . . . it also explains why Dad was so paranoid about me cleaning my cricket boots!

  These are the details you should consider including in your manuscript.

ASSIGNMENTS

- Write down your reasons for writing your life story. Don't worry if these change during the course of the project.

- Your book will be around long after you have gone and may well be read by people who never met you. Consider what you might write about yourself that will convey to such people the sort of person you are.

- If you are still unsure as to whether to embark on this project, write down your reservations and discuss them with a friend.

2

Defining the Project

There are many ways to record your life story and this chapter will help you decide what sort of project you might like to undertake.

Before proceeding further it is worth considering four factors:

- your audience
- what type of record you want
- whether you require any assistance
- your proposed style of writing.

KNOWING YOUR AUDIENCE

It is important that you are aware of your readership because the book will be shaped accordingly. For example, if your son has asked you to write you may consider it unnecessary to describe life in the East End of London after the war – after all, he was brought up there. However, not only will your viewpoints differ, even of the same event, but assumptions you make for him will not hold for every reader. What happens when a grandchild or a neighbour asks to read the book?

Such comparisons become even more stark if you have lived abroad. For those who know little or nothing about Colonial East Africa or wartime France an opportunity will have been lost to provide a fascinating read.

Thinking laterally

Once you have decided to embark on writing a book, it is worth thinking more widely. As memories of your childhood become ever more remote, so new generations will find it increasingly difficult to understand a secret language ... who will know what ten bob was in thirty years' time?

For the purposes of your life story it is best to assume little prior knowledge – or even none – so as to appeal to a wider audience. You can still include the family in-jokes, most of which will probably go unnoticed by the uninitiated. Where such references come across as a little odd, you may need to include a small explanation for those not 'in the know'.

Being diplomatic

For the sake of diplomacy it is also worth considering who might potentially read your book. If a close friend had written an autobiography you would undoubtedly be keen to find out if you were mentioned. The same will be true of those who read your book. The fact that you have sent someone a Christmas card for the last 43 years must mean something. Just a mention of their name and perhaps a sentence or two could save a lot of awkwardness if, and when, they come to read the book.

While it may be your intention that the book will only be read by the grandchildren, you will be amazed by how many people will ask to read it when they know that they have an author in their midst.

DECIDING WHAT TYPE OF RECORD YOU WANT

There are many ways to record the story of your life and being aware of the possibilities may lead to a more fulfilling, enjoyable and comprehensive project.

The labels themselves are not particularly important, especially as many of them become blurred. What does matter is that you know what type of record you want to achieve.

For convenience, the terms 'life story', 'biography' and 'autobiography' will be used interchangeably in this book, although the information will invariably apply to whatever project you decide to embark upon.

Here are some of your options:

Autobiography

This is the most common term used if you write your life story, and, by definition, is written by the subject of the book.

Alternative structures are suggested in Chapter 5, but usually an autobiography will flow chronologically, beginning with what the author knows of his or her immediate ancestors. The author is then introduced and the account of his or her life follows.

Joint autobiography

This may sound like a contradiction but is, in fact, a very popular way of presenting the life stories of two or more people – usually a married couple. Each partner writes an account that either stands side by side or is woven into the book. Assuming that both partners are equally enthusiastic, this can be an immensely enjoyable project.

Another variation is for one partner to undertake the majority of the writing, while the other provides the occasional few pages.

Several sample frameworks for such projects can be found in Chapter 5.

Biography

Such a book is written by a third party (or ghostwriter) either with or without the permission of the subject. The lives of the famous are often ghostwritten, and even books claiming to be autobiographies are often written 'with assistance'. The quality of these vary enormously.

There is nothing wrong with ghostwritten books, but it is rare to find one that fully encapsulates the character of the subject. We tend to write the way we speak and our own book will reflect this. Our character and mannerisms will shine through, something which is very hard for anyone else to capture.

The term 'biography' is often used generically to refer to the diverse area of life story and reminiscence, including autobiography.

Joint biography

This is where more than one third party writes about the subject of the book.

Some people ask their children to write an account of childhood to be included either in the main body of the book or as an appendix. Again, sample frameworks for such projects can be found in Chapter 5.

Memoir

Sometimes used interchangeably with the words 'biography' and 'autobiography', a memoir tends to be a collection of anecdotes rather than a detailed chronological history.

You may remember little about your childhood, or do not want to write about it for one reason or another, but hopefully that will not deflect you from writing snippets about the rest of your life. Characters you have known, stories from your national service days, anecdotes from your career, hobbies, parenthood and dozens of other subjects all make for an excellent memoir.

Q: I only want to write about my childhood, but I have a few articles and some poetry – is it worth doing?

A: The project is well worth undertaking simply for the satisfaction that you will derive from it, quite apart from the joy it will give to others close to you. The information contained within this book applies whether you are writing about a small part of your life or all of it. Additionally, suggestions as to how you might present poetry, letters, articles, documents, etc. can be found in Chapter 12. Your intended project is just as valid as any other.

Diary or journal

This is probably the purest and most intimate form of autobiography. You may have been keeping a diary for years, or have just begun. Whether this is kept as a private record or is made public, and if so in what detail, is entirely up to you. However, if you are of a particularly candid disposition and are outspoken in your opinions, the reference to libel in Chapter 10 might best be borne in mind. What you write in private may need some editing before it is suitable for a wider readership.

Family history

While this sounds imposing, it can be an autobiography with a stronger emphasis on the wider family than might otherwise be the case. In its more formal guise, the family history can be a well-researched and thorough document with leanings towards genealogy.

Q: Do I have to include the dates of all my ancestors?

A: If there are only a few it does no harm, but if your grandmother was one of 13 it could get a little tedious. The important detail is that she, with her twin sister Mabel (born three minutes earlier the other side of midnight), was one of 13 born over a span of 16 years from 1895. The twins were born in 1904, had three older brothers and two older sisters, and there was another set of twins later – Arthur and Betty. Your favourite was Aunt Tootles (Winifred – don't know why she was called Tootles!). Also, in his final years Uncle Frank lived with you, with that infernal dog of his called Norman. You know nothing of the others.

   If you have all the dates of birth you may as well use them – they will be particularly useful for any genealogist in the family. However, to stop the narrative becoming tedious you could list the dates in a table, include them in an appendix or produce a family tree.

Genealogy

Genealogical research is pursued with great dedication by many amateur and professional enthusiasts. As plenty of guidance is readily available elsewhere, research methods will not be discussed here.

The findings of such research can fit easily within the framework of a family book, although care has to be taken not to create an imbalance. With this in mind, lists of raw data and census returns might better be encompassed within an appendix unless the book is a pure genealogical record.

Sticking to what you know
This book focuses primarily upon living memories – what we recall and what is readily to hand rather than any detailed research. A chat with Great Aunt Maud may well provide a treasure trove of stories about Grandma's childhood. Documents will still be available in public record offices long after Great Aunt Maud and her precious memories are gone.

CASE STUDY – Grandpa becomes side-tracked

Isabelle, Joseph and James asked Grandpa to write a few memories for them about his schooldays. Grandpa had often pointed out his old school as they had passed in the car – there had only been two classes and the school had long since been converted into a house. They also wanted to hear more about what he remembered of his parents and the mischief he'd got up to.

Grandpa took the view that a job worth doing was worth doing well and attacked the project with gusto. After he had been to a few museums and devoured several excellent reference books, Grandpa decided that before he put pen to paper he would do a bit of research into his ancestry. He was soon bitten by the genealogy bug and wanted to go back further and further. Each time he thought he was getting to the point where he would start his own writing, a new line of enquiry emerged and off he went.

Isabelle, Joseph and James will inherit files full of census returns and dates and names of distant ancestors dating back to the eighteenth century, and no doubt much earlier if Grandpa has his way. Sadly, they still know no more about their great-grandparents, Grandpa's school and the mischief he got up to as a lad.

Novel

It is well recognised that most first novels are heavily autobiographical. It stands to reason that we write about what we know best and draw from experience.

Be careful if this is your preferred presentation; thinly disguised characterisations can cause ill-feeling by those who suspect they are the subjects . . . not least because it is difficult to separate fact from fiction.

Pictorial presentation

For those with extensive collections of photographs and other templates and with little desire to write extensively, a pictorial presentation of your life is a sound option. This can be presented in a photograph album or other special volume. Alternatively, sophisticated reproduction methods allow for copies to be produced in a cost-effective manner. Further details can be found in Chapter 12.

Obviously, any information you have about the pictures will be a great bonus, and, who knows, it might encourage you to take the plunge and write your life story.

Collaborative ventures

In all the above, apart from perhaps the diary, it is possible for others to contribute to the book. This will usually be your partner, but there is no reason why it should not be a sibling, a cousin, or even a child or grand-child . . . a whole family celebration.

CASE STUDY – Including the whole family

While sorting through some family archives, Julia found a diary written by her father during the Great War. She knew he had written one, but had never seen it. Julia was mesmerised as she read about her father's time in the Camel Corps in Egypt and wanted to reproduce his diary for the family.

Knowing that there was not enough material for a book, Julia decided to write about her childhood and early life before she was married. She was able to encourage her two children to do the same, and even the five grandchildren wrote a couple of pages each. A few pictures and a leather binding enhanced the overall presentation and now *Four Generations of the Lloyd Family* resides in pride of place in Julia's bookcase.

Being aware of opportunities offered by technology

While this book will primarily concentrate on the written record and presentation in book-form, this is not your only option. A *sound archive* can be considered, which has the benefit of preserving voices, with all their inherent character, for posterity.

Recording can be undertaken in isolation, but there is nothing wrong with someone asking you questions and their voice also being heard. In either case, preparatory notes on the topics to be covered will help.

Tapes can later be transcribed and printed by a friend or a local secretarial service to form the basis of a book if that is your desire. Of course, the reverse is also true: having written your life story, you might also enjoy reading it onto tape.

A video record takes this idea a step further, and for those with a flair for technology, there is nothing to stop you setting up your own *website* on the Internet with regular updates. The possibilities are endless.

THE SCOPE OF THIS BOOK

This book will focus on the autobiography written chronologically in book form. As this is the most exhaustive work, you can pick and choose what subsets you require. If you feel that the years up until the time you started work were largely unimportant (assuming I cannot convinced you otherwise!), then begin your story there. Even if you do this, a few early details may be helpful. The reader likes to have some background, for example:

- where you lived
- how many siblings you had
- your education
  etc.

This can be most revealing at a later date if patterns emerge . . . even if you have not been able to recognise them yourself.

CONSIDERING EXTERNAL ASSISTANCE

Writing your life story is a large undertaking and some external help and advice might be useful. Hopefully, having read this book you will feel equipped for most eventualities and will even be setting your own milestones. However, sharing these targets and having someone act as a sounding board might be beneficial, particularly if you come to a difficult part in the story.

You will find that chatting about your childhood with someone else, preferably someone who knows little of your life and can therefore make no assumptions, leads to a whole host of ideas pouring forth. One idea triggers another, and before you know it you will have recalled memories you thought were long since gone.

Even if you have decided on a joint book with your partner, it does not necessarily follow that he or she will be the best person to offer objective advice, particularly if you never stop talking about the project!

Finding a writing partner

Various opportunities are open to you:

- a family member . . . maybe a sibling or an in-law
- a trusted friend
- a recommendation from a local writers' group
- enrolment in a life writing class – many local authorities offer them
- enrolment on an adult education/university course
- assistance from a professional writing partner.

Some useful contacts can be found at the back of this book.

Setting up a life writing class

If a class is not offered by your local authority, you might like to set up your own. Two or three friends, a local advert and word of mouth will soon establish a small group. A couple of hours a week is all that is required . . . and it's great fun.

SELECTING YOUR WRITING STYLE

Writing in the first person

Most life stories are written in the first person. Initially, you might find it difficult using the word 'I' so much, but it is hard to avoid and you will soon start to feel comfortable with this style. A well-written life story will sound like the author is speaking, and in speech the word 'I' is totally acceptable.

A book written in the third person sounds stilted and uncomfortable. Unless you have very strong reasons for adopting this practice, it is not recommended.

Knowing your audience

Your style will largely be dictated by your audience. You might choose to adopt a chatty style, or perhaps prefer to be more formal if the book is intended for a wider audience, for example former work colleagues.

Feeling comfortable

In most cases you will slip into a certain style without thinking about it, just as if you were writing a letter. It is important that you feel comfortable with how you write and do not over-analyse it. Just be yourself.

It is difficult to contrive a style. For example, if you are not noted for your humour, it is unlikely that your book will be a laugh a minute, but that won't make it any less enjoyable for the reader. If you try to act out of character and be someone you are not the book might be a disappointment to those who know and love you.

Being yourself

Interestingly, men and women tend to write different sorts of books. As a rule, women are very open and are far more comfortable about including everything in their book, 'warts and all'. Men have a tendency to be more conservative, being less inclined to share thoughts and feelings. This is probably a reflection of society; men are not encouraged to share at such an intimate level – women do it with their female friends all the time.

While these are observations gleaned from working with scores of people at an intimate level, they are a generalisation; individuals will fall into the different categories.

Ultimately, there is no right or wrong way. The choice is yours . . . this is your book.

CHOOSING A TITLE

There is no need to finalise the title for a long while yet, but you might want to choose a provisional title for your book so that the project seems all the more real. If you haven't given your title any thought, you might like to consider something intriguing to catch attention, rather than 'The Life Story of Joe Soap' or 'I did it my way'.

Drawing upon a theme from your life is a good starting point, perhaps a reference to your career. For example, 'Tending to Care' was written by a nurse, while 'A Balance Sheet of Life' was the work of an accountant.

Other ideas are:

- A quotation   – Unto the Breach Dear Friends
- Something intriguing   – No Pie on Payday
- A family saying   – Catch Yourself on Mrs
- A verse from the Bible   – They Shall Inherit the Earth

- A song title   – Don't Forget to Remember
- A favourite hymn   – The Wings of a Dove

One lady writing the book as a tribute to her late husband called it, 'The Gospel according to John's Wife', while another chap with the surname Buss, called his 'Move Along Please!'

You can have great fun with this, but don't worry if nothing immediately springs to mind; something is likely to come to you during the writing of the book.

CHECKLIST

- Who is going to read your book?

- What type of record are you looking to produce?

- Are you writing on your own or is it a joint book?

- Do you require any external assistance?

ASSIGNMENTS

- If you already have a title in mind, write it down.

- Write the introduction to your book explaining why you are writing, who it is for and what you intend to include. This will be revised later, but the exercise will help you to focus on what you want; it will also help you to feel comfortable with your writing style.

3

Preparation

By now you should know:

- that you want to write
- who the book is for
- whether this is to be a solo or joint project
- the type of project you require.

However, before your enthusiasm carries you away, it is important to get organised.

CHOOSING YOUR WRITING MEDIUM

Writing in longhand

Using a pen and paper is the easiest, most versatile and potentially most creative way to write. You can write where you want and when you want – in the garden, on your lap whilst watching snooker on TV, or even at three o'clock in the morning in bed . . . assuming you have a tolerant partner!

Millions of books have been written in longhand and, whatever anyone says about modern technology, this will undoubtedly be the formula for millions more.

The most important thing is to complete the manuscript. Once written, it is easy to get it typed. There is nothing wrong with a photo-copied handwritten manuscript in a ring binder, but with so many options available you will probably prefer a presentation that is easier on the eye.

Plenty of suggestions for presentation are provided in Chapter 12. If you are intending to leave the manuscript in a handwritten format, it is certainly worth reading that chapter first . . . unless you want to rewrite it all.

Q: My handwriting is terrible – will I have to write it out again before I send it to a typist?

A: The general rule of thumb is that if you can read it, so can a typist. They are used to all sorts of scrawl and certainly do not expect a work of art.

     If there are some particularly bad bits, like the anecdote you wrote in bed after a dinner party with friends, then you might want to rewrite it, but otherwise it should be all right. If you use a shorthand, like writing 'E' for your friend Elizabeth and 'NCL' for Newcastle, you will need to provide a key. Writing proper names in block capitals is also helpful.

Tapping on a typewriter

If your typewriter is your trusted friend, then by all means use it. It may be slightly less flexible than pen and paper, but if sitting at your typewriter is where you feel at your most creative, then this is the tool for you.

Bear in mind that certain forms of presentation may require your manuscript to be word processed at a later stage. Again, please refer to Chapter 12.

Using a word processor

Many people love their word processor and wonder how they ever managed without it. They feel inspired, creative, liberated. If this is you, then your choice has already been made.

Word processors can be a dedicated machine or a word processing program on a computer. In either case it is worth ensuring that yours is compatible with modern systems, or at least that there is an upgrade path. It is sometimes difficult making disks from older systems work with modern printers, which could cause headaches when it comes to printing your book. Some investigation early on could save much anguish later.

If you are familiar with an older word processor, you will be pleasantly surprised how easy the newer systems are to use, but it still might be worth a few lessons. Most adult education colleges offer word processing courses for total beginners. These are often subsidised or even free. Your local library or adult education college will be happy to offer advice.

CASE STUDY – Asif gives up in frustration

Asif was full of enthusiasm as he began to write the story of his life, a project he had been considering for years. He had made a solid start when a friend suggested he buy a word processor. Asif, forever one to do things properly, immediately went along to his local computer shop to investigate things further. He met a very enthusiastic young man and before he knew it, Asif came away with an all-singing all-dancing wonder machine. It was a bit more than he had intended to pay, but he was assured that it would do everything he ever wanted.

For the next five months Asif persevered with his new toy, but however much he read the manual, he just felt that he was going backwards. Jasbinder tried to encourage him by suggesting that he go to a class at the local college, but Asif would not be defeated.

The wonder machine now sits in the spare room gathering dust . . . along with the first two and a half chapters of Asif's manuscript.

Knowing your limits

If you are unfamiliar with word processors, please consider carefully before deciding to write your life story with one. For every person who is a fanatical convert to computers there are those who shudder at the very thought of using them.

If you want to learn to use a word processor, a good time is when it comes to reviewing and editing your manuscript. At least if you do give up, the all-important information has already been captured.

Recording onto tape

For those for whom writing is difficult, or if you feel particularly comfortable with tape recorders, this could be the perfect medium for you. It also has the added benefit of retaining a record of your voice for posterity, something that will delight future generations in years to come.

Dictating your life story requires discipline in terms of preparing notes beforehand. It is also wise to keep a list of the subjects covered on each tape and in which order – if only to know where to add a stray anecdote if the tapes are transcribed. The tapes should be given reference numbers, and annotated to show the years covered and the date the recording was made.

Making the decision

You may well choose a combination of the above. Indeed, if you use a word processor, a typewriter or a tape recorder, it is likely that you will still make notes in longhand.

Ultimately you should choose the medium with which you feel the most comfortable and creative.

FINDING YOUR OWN SPECIAL PLACE

Getting comfortable

People differ as to where they like to work; some rove around as the whim takes them, others prefer always to be in the same place. However, even for the itinerant, it is worth having a base – your own special place to keep your manuscript, notes and any memorabilia you collect.

Writing is going to occupy much of your time over the coming months, so if you can set a room aside, so much the better. This will also allow you to leave notes and pictures spread out to inspire you when it comes to your next session.

Remaining undisturbed

Find a place where you can reminisce and let your mind wander undisturbed. It is worth making this area personal to you, a place where you want to work – a comfy chair, good lighting, perhaps the odd picture or two and plenty of writing materials so that you don't have to run off and find another pen just as the words are starting to flow.

Q: I don't want to tell anyone that I'm writing a book until it is finished. Is this possible?

A: It might be hard to keep your writing a secret from anyone with whom you share a house, but others should present few problems. Some cunning may be required if information or pictures are required from those sources not in the know, but this should not be difficult . . . after all, they have no idea that you are writing a book.

Not telling too many people about it also avoids you being asked, "How's the book coming along?" After several months this can become quite tiresome. A secret book also provides a wonderful excuse for a surprise 'launch'.

GETTING ORGANISED

Setting up a simple filing system

Once you start reminiscing you will be amazed how the floodgates open. It is important that these precious pieces of information are not lost. A simple filing system can save a lot of grief later . . . especially if it means you don't lose any treasured photos you may have borrowed.

As it is worth collating the information in chapters, a concertina file might come in useful. However, a number of large envelopes or some box files will do just as well. One author even collected cardboard tomato boxes from the local supermarket. The protruding corners made for easy stacking – they were ideal . . . all 21 of them!

Having the right tools for the job

Once you have decided to write your life story, it is worth keeping several notepads around the house, especially on the bedside table. You can guarantee that just as you are about to nod off to sleep some fascinating detail will filter into your mind . . . the subconscious is amazing like that. You then either spend a sleepless night trying to ensure you don't forget it, or you torture yourself in the morning trying to remember what was so earth shattering. Write it down.

It is also worth keeping some paper and a pen on you at all times, just in case a random comment at the bus stop sparks off another flash of inspiration. A notepad and pen in the car is also a useful idea.

Spoiling yourself

Some people like to buy a special pen and a good quality notebook, the latter acting as a master reference for all the notepads around the house and for any inspirational ideas. A hardback book in which to write the actual manuscript is not advisable – a lever-arch file and loose-leaf sheets allow greater flexibility in adding information at a later stage.

Being prepared

Office superstores provide great value and are well worth a visit to stock up on useful items for the project. These might include:

- notepads
- lined A4 pads (preferably with margins and pre-punched holes)
- pens
- pencils
- rubber
- treasury tags

- paper clips
- coloured highlighter pens
- lever-arch file
- concertina file for pictures and documents (box file and envelopes will suffice)
- dividers
- hole punch.

If you are using a word processor and printer ensure you have back-up disks and a spare cartridge, for a typewriter a spare ribbon, and for both plenty of paper.

Establishing a back-up system
Even if you are writing the manuscript in longhand or using a typewriter it is worth thinking about taking a photocopy. This is particularly important if you send a chapter or two to a friend to proofread, or perhaps to your brother to check a few facts about your early life. However, even a wayward cup of coffee, a hungry dog or an over-exuberant grandchild can soon put paid to many hours of work.

Backing-up your word processor
If your writing is on computer, back-ups become all the more essential. Modern systems can back up at pre-specified intervals, for example every ten minutes, without any interference to the user. This is worthwhile in case you inadvertently forget to save the file or there is a system crash. Having to retype hours of work is frustrating to say the least.

A back-up of the files used every session is good practice. It may even be worth keeping a spare back-up disk with a neighbour and swapping it every week or two for further peace of mind.

SETTING PROVISIONAL TARGETS

Recognising how you work
You may be the sort of person who likes to set time aside regularly or you might attack the project in bursts and then leave it for several weeks before recommencing. Summer is a busy time for some and so they undertake the bulk of the writing between autumn and early spring. Then there are the 'morning people', whilst others prefer to burn the midnight oil. Work to your strengths.

Booking time to write

Some people find booking time in their diary a useful discipline as events can easily eat into the time earmarked for writing. An 'appointment' in the diary can make time spent writing more official.

Finding time to write in the early stages when there is enthusiasm by the bucketful will not be a problem, but once deep into the project it can be a different matter. Most writers recognise that some discipline is important to overcome the difficult times.

This project is meant to be enjoyable, not a chore, so be realistic in your planning. It does not matter if your manuscript takes longer to complete than anticipated . . . as long as it gets completed. Recognise your strengths and weaknesses and plan accordingly.

Allowing thinking time

You are likely to be thinking about this project for a great many of your waking hours, especially early on . . . sometimes to the frustration of those around you! Mulling things over in your mind is a vital part of the process and so if you don't write much in some of the sessions you have set aside, don't worry about it. Just because you are not writing, does not mean you are not working.

Having a launch date in mind

Although it is hard to estimate how long the project will take, some people like to have a timescale in mind; a provisional target for the launch of the book can help focus the mind.

Q: How long will it take me to write?

A: Once inspired, some people sit down and write reams, completing a comprehensive record in as little as three or four months. For others the research alone can take much longer and they work on their book for years.

For those setting aside one or two sessions a week, a year is a realistic target in which to write and edit a manuscript. Depending on the type of presentation you require, especially if pictures are to be included, a further few months could be added to the schedule.

As projects often take much longer than expected, if you are thinking of finishing your book for your 68th birthday, it might also be worth considering your Ruby Wedding Anniversary eight months later as a fall-back date.

Establishing bite-sized chunks

If you decide to work towards a target date you can break the project down into manageable sections. This will be much easier to do after the brainstorming in Chapter 4 when you decide chapter headings.

CHECKLIST

- Do you feel comfortable with the writing medium you have chosen? You don't want to get deflected in your resolve to write . . . you will encounter enough distractions without adding one more.

- Have you collated the various materials you are going to need, and organised a place to keep these and all the memorabilia which will soon be descending upon you?

- If you have a deadline for the book, is it realistic?

ASSIGNMENTS

- Decide what targets are most likely to motivate you and help you in this project – maybe a certain number of hours or pages of writing a week. If the discipline helps, allocate some time in your diary for writing.

- Read a few autobiographies, not necessarily of famous people. This will give you some idea of the sort of book you might like. Interestingly, badly written books can teach you more as they show you what to avoid.

4

Planning the Structure

Planning the framework for your book and establishing chapter headings is surprisingly easy and enjoyable. A well spent hour or two here will provide an excellent provisional structure.

Please don't expect everything to be perfect first time. The structure will be continually revised throughout the course of the project, and can even be reviewed again once the manuscript has been written.

For ease of analysis, the structure here is written from the viewpoint of a single life story followed chronologically. Ideas for alternative structures and joint books are discussed in the next chapter.

DEFINING THE PARAMETERS OF THE BOOK

Deciding where to start

When you were considering the sort of record you wanted, you may have had an idea of where the book should begin. Techniques like flashbacks and turning points are covered in Chapter 7, but unless you have strong views to the contrary, describing what you know of your ancestors is always a good place to start.

You may feel that you know relatively little about your family background, but what you do know is likely to be of great interest to future generations. The countries from where the family originated or lived for many years, the industries in which they worked, the size of the families, social class and religion can all help to set the scene, particularly as families now tend to be smaller and more mobile.

There is no need to embark on any in-depth research just yet, although if a great uncle is still around it would certainly be worth finding out what he knows. It is invariably the case that most people know far more about their families than they appreciate or consider important.

The other popular place to start is with the birth of the author . . . 'I was born at home in the small hours of the morning on . . .' Of course, even with this it is possible to reflect back on the sort of family into which you were born.

Deciding where to finish

Most people like to bring their writing up to the present day, but you may have another milestone in mind, for example the millennium, your 50th wedding anniversary, the birth of your last grandchild, or your 75th birthday at the end of next year. Greater attention will be given to endings in Chapter 10.

The proposed end point of the book may well alter during the writing of your manuscript. With this in mind it is usually worth bringing your story up to the present when thinking about your chapter headings.

Q: How long should the book be?

A: There are no hard and fast rules – stop writing whenever you feel that you've said enough. However, it is worth being aware of false modesty – for the time being, simply write anything and everything.

A typical book will usually be between 40,000 and 80,000 words, about 150–300 pages. However, don't feel daunted. This only equates to 15–30 pages per chapter, and once you get going you will be amazed at how much you write.

If you are intending to have the book bound, you should be aiming for at least 150 sides, although the inclusion of pictures and a few introductory pages will account for some of these.

IDENTIFYING CHAPTER HEADINGS

Once you have established where you want the book to start and finish you are ready to jot down some chapter headings for your initial book structure. These are purely to help you categorise broad areas of your life, and might be as shown in Figure 1.

Typically there might be 10 or 15 categories that, by and large, cover the main areas of your life. As these categories should be obvious, there is no reason why this phase of the process should take more than ten minutes – half an hour at the outside.

If you have a CV, even a very old one, it could be very helpful here.

Family background
Childhood and schooldays
The war years
My first job
National Service
Back to work
Marriage
Early married life
Changing career
The family grows
Retirement
Grandchildren
Voluntary work

Fig. 1.   Initial book structure.

Breaking down the chapters

Obviously huge areas have been ignored and others do not fit comfortably under any heading, for example, friends, holidays, hobbies and pets, all of which may overlap several chapters.

Even at this stage you will probably be able to subdivide some headings, like 'Childhood', for example, if you moved several times, were evacuated or perhaps lived overseas.

A large category such as 'Family Life' covering a span of 30 years or more, might be better divided into two chapters entitled 'Early Married Life' and 'The Family Grows'. Of course, references to the children are also likely to appear in other chapters as well, although how much you include about them will be covered in greater length in Chapter 10. A long and diverse working life may well also require several chapters.

Q: How many years should a typical chapter cover?
A: This depends on how interesting the period is that you are considering. For example, if you were evacuated, even though this might have been for only 18 months, a separate chapter would be appropriate. There will be so much to relate, not least how you adjusted to the upheaval, and a description of your new and strange environment. In later life when there tend to be more set routines, a chapter can cover twenty years or more.

You will normally have a feel for significant areas in your life which justify a chapter in their own right. If an imbalance exists it is likely to be ironed out as you are writing – you will feel that you have come to a natural chapter break. Other concerns can be addressed when the book is reviewed for balance at the end.

BRAINSTORMING

This is where the creative process begins as you mentally trawl through your life and let the ideas flow.

Write each of your chapter headings on a separate sheet of paper. Then, concentrating on one of the headings, write down whatever topics come to mind. They don't have to be in any order.

For some headings there might only be three or four topics listed; for others there may be dozens. For the latter category, rewrite the list grouping common areas together, possibly under a general heading. This might look something like Figure 2.

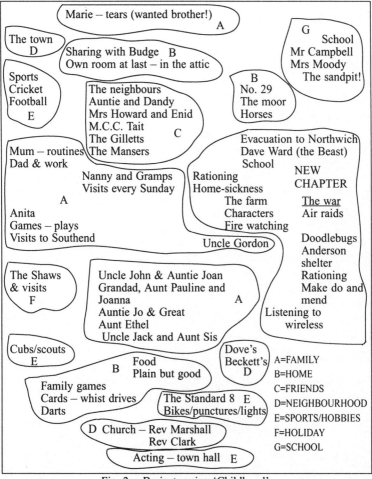

Fig. 2.   Brainstorming 'Childhood'.

Keeping focused

During this brainstorming you will undoubtedly be bombarded with detailed memories. It helps if you can capture the essence of your thoughts in just a few words because we think 12 times faster than we write!

What you are really looking for here are broad topics, but it is important that no precious recollections are lost. If specific memories flit into your mind, jot them down and then move on, concentrating on the more general areas. There will be an opportunity for more detailed brainstorming before you start writing the manuscript.

REVISING THE INITIAL BOOK STRUCTURE

These topics from Figure 2 can now be incorporated into the initial book structure (Figure 1) to produce Figure 3.

— Family background
      Parents in service at Cliveden
      Mum's family
      Dad's family
      Their childhoods and how they met

— Childhood + school days
      Family
      Home
      Friends
      Neighbourhood
      School
      Sports/hobbies
      Holidays

— Evacuation
      Dad departing
      Air raids
      Changes encountered
      Rationing
      School + friends
      Countryside

— Return to London
      Devastation
      Home (new)
      School
      Scouts

Fig. 3. Section of revised book structure.

In the above example the chapter dealing with the war has been divided into two chapters entitled 'Evacuation' and 'Return to London'.

We are aiming at balance throughout the book, but this won't necessarily emerge immediately because at this stage we cannot tell how long each section will be. However, beware of 17 chapters about work and only one on the family . . . and that one including golf and holidays!

Remaining organised

You may find that you have made many more notes than those transcribed onto the revised book structure. It is important that these are not lost. Place these sheets of paper in your filing system for future reference – you haven't finished with the book structure yet!

INTRODUCING A TIME LINE

Against this revised book structure you can add a time line to map dates to the framework. This helps to organise facts and reduce the risk of omitting significant areas.

Some dates will spring readily to mind:

- birth
- years at school
- starting work
- marriage
  etc.

Other dates may need a little more thought:

- births of three younger brothers
- visiting Bob in Canada
- meeting your partner
- buying first car
- Jim dying
- being promoted to section leader
  etc.

It is not essential that all dates be precise, the general period is enough . . . although with something like your wedding day someone else may appreciate you getting it right!

CASE STUDY – Slapdash Terry

Terry had always been someone who got stuck right in when it came to starting a new project: 'Strike while the iron's hot' was his motto. Eileen wished he paid more attention to preparation – perhaps the kitchen units might shut properly if he did!

When it came to writing his life story, Terry was right in there as usual – despite Eileen's suggestion that a few notes in advance might not be a bad idea. He may only have been a literary Lilliputian, but the first four or five chapters simply fell out of Terry's pen. Eileen was a little concerned on several occasions when she wondered aloud if Terry had mentioned a particular episode, only to see him scurrying to his den. But, by and large, the manuscript was progressing well.

The real problem came when Terry had to lay his writing aside for three months. He had not lost enthusiasm, it was just that the grandchildren stayed for three weeks, then there was his knee replacement operation followed by a holiday . . .

Terry did eventually finish his writing. However, by now he was bored with the project and couldn't be bothered to review it. He had it bound, and in fact it was not a bad effort, but Eileen knew that it was somewhat higgledy-piggledy and could have been so much better . . . and she had to bite her tongue when she noticed that he'd forgotten to mention his brother George.

Adding key historical dates

You can also include key dates of history which come into your story and which help you place where you were. We are only looking at major events here, those that come readily to mind and dates that trip off the tongue. A more detailed analysis comes later.

Such events might include:

- 1939 – war started (September)
- 1945 – war ended (May Europe – August Japan)
- 1947 – severe winter freeze
- 1948 – NHS founded (Betty training as nurse)
- 1952 – King George VI dies
- 1953 – Coronation (got our first TV set)
- 1956 – Clean Air Act (living in London – smog!)
  etc.

WEAVING IT ALL TOGETHER

Figure 4 shows part of the fully revised book structure, including the time line.

Some subject areas fit neatly in one chapter while others span several. Ideas for dealing with overlapping subjects are considered in the next chapter.

	Year	My age
— Family background	pre 1930	
Parents in service at Cliveden		
Mum's family		
Dad's family		
Their childhoods and how they met		
— Childhood + school days	1930–9	0–9
Family		
Home		
Friends		
Neighbourhood		
School		
Sports/hobbies		
Holidays		
— Evacuation	1939–42	9–12
Dad departing		
Air raids	1940	
Changes encountered		
Rationing	1940–54	
School + friends		
Countryside		
— Return to London	1942–5	12–15
Devastation		
Home (new)		
School		
Scouts		
Doodlebugs	1944	
VE Day	1945 (May 8th)	

Fig. 4. Integrated structure with time line and historical dates.

TAKING A BREAK

You can feel satisfied that on a few sheets of paper you have the essence of your book . . . now all you have to do is break down each chapter into much more detail and then write the manuscript! However, all that can come later. Your head is probably spinning too much to consider doing anything more just yet. Relax – you've earned it.

CHECKLIST

- Are you happy with your start and end points?

- Are you confident that your book structure covers all the major episodes you want to include?

- Think about friends and family who might potentially read the book. Have you included something about each of them?

ASSIGNMENTS

- Look at other autobiographies and see how the books are structured and what material is included.

- Consider asking someone who knows you well to review the intended structure of your book.

5

Considering Alternative Structures

This chapter provides ideas for different book structures and how to accommodate other contributions.

THINKING LATERALLY

You can be creative in how you structure your book. A few of the more conventional ideas are listed here, but feel free to let your mind wander.

Expressing your life in time spans

The early years of our life can usually be associated with certain ages. The following would be an example:

0–5	Pre-school and family background
5–11	Primary and junior schools
11–16	Secondary school
16–18	Early working life
18–21	National Service
21–25	Meeting Mary and settling down
25–30	Early married life and children.

If this pattern can be followed relatively neatly throughout the later stages of your life as well, you might like to consider structuring your writing in this way.

Using the decades

A variation on the above theme is to write your book in decades. These can either be the decades of your life or of the twentieth century:

My life	*The twentieth century*
Early years	1930s
My teens	1940s
My twenties	1950s
My thirties	1960s
etc.	etc.

Placing your life in specific compartments

The methods expressed so far have been consistent with a chronological approach to writing your life story. If you want something a little more adventurous you could consider writing in various compartments each spanning the whole of your life:

Jim the student
Jim the family man
Jim the working man
Jim the friend
Jim the sportsman
Jim the traveller
Jim the poet

Unless there are several quite distinct areas of your life, this is probably not a recommended structure. However, these ideas might help you to think more laterally about your own project.

Mixing structures

Of course, even within the more conventional chronological book structure, there is nothing to stop you introducing creative chapters. You might want to write about 'The Swinging Sixties', 'Life in my Thirties' or 'My Thespian Career'. Alternatively, you can include a 'Soapbox' where you put the world to rights, or perhaps have a more reflective, 'What If . . .' chapter.

UNDERTAKING A JOINT PROJECT

There is no limit on the options available to you or the number of contributors to a book. For example, seven brothers and sisters can each write a chapter for a family archive. Cousins, business partners or friends joining forces provide other options.

Such projects tend to have a simple structure with each contributor writing either a chapter or section of the book.

There is greater scope for interweaving chapters when the book is written by a married couple, or by different generations of a family.

WRITING AS A COUPLE

This is a very popular project for those who enjoy working closely together. Having a sounding board and someone else who can share the joys and frustrations of writing is a great benefit. Additionally, such a book tends to be more well-rounded, capturing the personalities of both parties.

There are two main types of project you might like to consider here:

- equal partnership
- one partner taking the lead.

Contributing as equal partners

Each partner will write about their background, childhood and early life before they met. Once their lives join together, the subsequent chapters will be written by either party. Some subjects like children and work will probably fall quite neatly into place, but decisions will have to be made as to who writes about holidays, grandchildren, etc.

Of course, there is no reason why certain subjects should not be written about by both partners. Indeed, for events like when you first met it can be fascinating to read accounts from two different viewpoints.

Q: My husband and I are working on a joint book. How much should we confer about our writing?

A: For subjects that clearly have to be written by one partner, like early childhood, it may help to discuss ideas to stimulate the memory. Where you are writing about the same subject, for example your wedding day, it is better to write independently as the interest often lies in the difference of recollections and emphasis. However, this can lead to some disappointment . . . for example, the man who described the highlight of his wedding day as seeing a peregrine falcon on the way to the church!

Weaving the book together

The two most popular ways of interspersing chapters can be seen in Figures 5 and 6.

Bill	–	Meet the ancestors
Dot	–	In the beginning . . .
Bill	–	Childhood
Dot	–	Life in India
Dot	–	Coming to England
Bill	–	Schooldays
Dot	–	Schooling in Malvern
Dot	–	Back to India
Bill	–	Apprenticeship
Bill	–	National Service
Dot	–	Training as a nurse
Bill	–	Holt Industries
Dot	–	Qualified
Bill	–	The cycling club
Bill	–	Meeting Dorothy
Dot	–	Bill

The two lives coming together

Dot	–	Early married life
Bill	–	Going solo
Bill	–	Forming ACA
Dot	–	The family grows
Bill	–	Selling up
Bill	–	Moving to the Lake District
Dot	–	Round the world
Dot	–	Grandchildren
Bill	–	What next?

Fig. 5. Contributing to chapters – method 1.

As can be seen, whichever structure is chosen, once the two lives come together the rest of the book follows the same format.

Of course, as with the sole author, the structure can be refined as you proceed; the only difference is that it involves a little communication.

If both partners choose to write their independent life stories there is no reason why the two accounts should not be placed after each other and bound in the same cover. However, this is not so much a joint autobiography, as two separate autobiographies produced in the same volume.

One partner taking the lead

While many couples are equally enthusiastic about the prospect of writing, more often than not the passion for the project is weighted

```
                    Bill  —  Meet the ancestors
                             Childhood
                             Schooldays
                             Apprenticeship
                             National Service
                             Holt Industries
                             The cycling club
                             Meeting Dorothy
                    Dot  —  In the beginning . . .
                             Life in India
                             Coming to England
                             Schooling in Malvern
                             Back to India
                             Training as a nurse
                             Qualified!
                             Bill


The two lives coming together
                    Dot  —  Early married life
                    Bill  —  Going solo
                    Bill  —  Forming ACA
                    Dot  —  The family grows
                    Bill  —  Selling up
                    Bill  —  Moving to the Lake District
                    Dot  —  Round the world
                    Dot  —  Grandchildren
                    Bill  —  What next?
```

Fig. 6.   Contributing to chapters – method 2.

heavily in favour of one of the parties. George might be writing his book, but Irene is happy to contribute a chapter about her early life for the benefit of the grandchildren.

In such a case, it is recommended that George structures the book as if he were doing it entirely by himself.

Tying in the partner's contribution
When George gets to the point in his story where he disappears off on honeymoon with Irene he might now write something along the lines of:

'Before I continue with our married life together, Irene has provided a few pages about her family and early life.'

Irene's chapter covering the time until she married George is then inserted, after which George continues with his book.

If Irene is happy to add some further material later, perhaps about the children in their early years, this can similarly be tied in at the appropriate stage in the narrative.

CASE STUDY – Ted changes his mind

Ted had always wanted to write about his days in the Merchant Marine – the 'wavy navy' as he called it. Beryl was happy to encourage him, not least as he was getting under her feet now that he had finally retired. She suggested that while he was at it, Ted might as well bring his story up to the present day.

Ted immersed himself in his new project and all went smoothly until it came to writing about the family. He had been away for much of the time when the children were growing up and did not know what to write. In a flash of inspiration Ted asked Beryl if she would write a few pages. Beryl was flattered, and wrote a chapter about the children – indeed she also wrote a second chapter about her early life to provide a balanced book for the grandchildren.

Ted was delighted . . . he even learned a few things about Beryl and the children in the process! All he had to do was rewrite the introduction to his book to explain the new format.

WRITING AS SEPARATE GENERATIONS

Asking the children to contribute

A person writing an autobiography might ask the children if they would like to contribute a few pages about their childhoods. These can then either be included within the body of the book, or alternatively as appendices, whichever is more appropriate. See Chapter 12 for ideas.

There is no reason why other members of the family, particularly siblings or grandchildren, should not be given a similar opportunity.

In this instance, the book is likely to be written by the grandparent with various small contributions from other family members.

Writing as a family

A more adventurous project might be for several family members to contribute to one book. They can decide their own content, or all write on the same subject. A title like 'My Childhood' would provide a fascinating record, especially among the different generations.

It may be that a grandparent acts as narrator for the book, providing the framework and introducing the various family members at the appropriate places.

Such a project needs strong coordination but is a hugely enjoyable and rewarding experience.

CHECKLIST

● Is there anything else you can add to the structure of your book?

● Is their anyone you might ask to contribute to your book?

ASSIGNMENT

● Review your book structure to see if it can be improved in the light of this chapter.

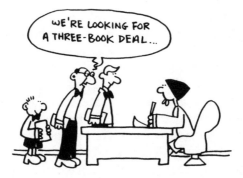

6

Preparing to Tell the Story

This chapter considers some writing points that you might like to bear in mind before putting pen to paper.

Don't try to digest everything – read through the chapter and then let ideas wander into your mind over the next few days. Perhaps after you've written a chapter or two you can revisit this chapter for more ideas, and again prior to reading through the entire manuscript before the final edit.

FEELING COMFORTABLE WITH YOURSELF

Being yourself

The most important advice in this whole chapter is for you to be yourself. People love us for being us, with all of our little imperfections and foibles. If in our writing we try to make ourselves out to be someone we are not, it will not ring true.

As this is likely to be a purely private book, those reading it will know you very well. You will remember some events differently from your readers – that is only to be expected. The memory also plays tricks from time to time. However, if the reader perceives that history is being rewritten on too many occasions your book will lose credibility.

Remember, your readers are on your side. Just be yourself.

Striking the right balance

Most people err on the side of modesty rather than arrogance. However, beware, a book dripping with humility can grate with the reader just as much as arrogance.

CASE STUDY – Frank's perfect marriage

Frank was a man's man. He lived life to the full and called a spade a spade. His marriage to Mollie had been a bit of a rumbustious affair, but they had muddled through, largely because Mollie knew when to bite her tongue. Frank had a bit of a temper as the neighbours well knew – the fact that he had been a drill sergeant in the army probably accounted for that.

When Mollie died, Frank decided it was time to write his life story. He was quite open and fair in most of what he wrote – he knew he was no saint. Strangely, though, his recollections of his marriage to Mollie differed quite significantly from those of his readers. The words 'idyllic', 'harmonious' and 'never a cross word . . .' did not automatically spring to their minds!

Sharing secrets

How much you choose to reveal about yourself is obviously up to you. However, sharing a secret with the reader, even a small one like a hitherto unknown nickname or an embarrassing moment from your childhood, will endear you to your audience.

Many high-profile biographies fall into the trap of keeping the reader at arm's length. Having reached the final page it is all too easy to feel that you know no more about the person than before you started.

BEING NATURAL

Writing the way you speak

CASE STUDY – Roy lives on

Prior to his death, Roy wrote his life story. In fact he had so enjoyed the experience that he even wrote a sequel. Each volume was quite large, but there again, Roy was never one to use one word where 27 would fit just as well.

In the address at his funeral, a few pages of Roy's first book were read to the congregation. Afterwards several people commented that they could hear Roy speaking through his book. Roy lives on.

As long as you are not trying to be too clever, you will easily fall into a comfortable writing style. The best way to achieve this is to write the way you speak.

The use of a thesaurus can add colour and diversity to your manuscript, but try not to use those words where you have to look up the meaning. If you don't even know what they mean they are clearly not in your everyday vocabulary.

Using humour
If you are humorous by nature, this will reflect in your writing. Anecdotes are the usual form of introducing humour, and a few well-chosen stories will add to your story. However, think carefully about what you write – once in print it's there forever . . . and what sounded like a good idea at the time might be a little insensitive.

Additionally, the odd tale against yourself will engage the reader and make it easier to tell a gentle story against someone else.

BEING THOROUGH

Not discounting anything
The usual adage about writing a book is that, come the end, the waste-paper basket is full of golden nuggets that failed to make the final cut. However, if they are golden nuggets why shouldn't they be included?

The fascination in a life story is the detail – the fact that a memory has jumped back into your consciousness after 50 or 60 years must mean something. Include it.

Substituting yourself with a grandparent
A useful test here is to substitute yourself with your grandmother or grandfather. If they had written a book, what would you want to know? The answer has surely got to be, 'Everything', or, at the very least, 'Whatever they chose to say.'

If your grandmother had confided the fact that her favourite colour was sky-blue and that as a child she had an imaginary friend called Boris, you'd be delighted. It might also explain your vivid imagination or why your favourite colour is sky-blue.

Leaving the editing for later
Just because you write something early on does not mean that it has to appear in the final book if, upon review, you feel that the narrative has become tedious. However, it is easier to make such decisions when you

consider the balance of the entire manuscript rather than a few pages at a time.

Obviously, boring your reader is something to be avoided, but care has to be exercised to ensure that it is not simply modesty speaking. Again, ask the question, 'What would you have wanted your grandfather to have eliminated from his writing?' At this stage, keep it in. Your readers can always skip pages if they wish – the odds are that they won't.

Editing will be discussed at greater length in Chapter 11 when it comes to reviewing your manuscript.

Assuming nothing

Whoever your intended audience, it is best to assume no knowledge by the reader. While your children are well aware of the fact that Grandpa had a wooden leg, what about the as yet unborn great-grandchild? Without the relevant knowledge, the story of Grandpa sawing off his leg when he trapped it in a cattle grid takes on a different meaning!

Providing a reference point

Increasingly fewer people know what ten bob was – how many less in 30 years' time? However, the fact that it is 50p is of less interest than providing a reference as to what that could buy. Your Dad was earning £3.15s.0d a week at the time . . . and he was manager of the local cinema in charge of 12 staff.

Similarly, everyone knows that Gordon was your best mate, but mentioning that you met on a works outing to the Isle of Wight adds a bit of background to someone who virtually became one of the family. If Gordon suddenly appears in the story from nowhere it might confuse some potential future readers.

Of course, not everything can be explained, and if Vera Lynn is not known in 50 years' time at least it might make the reader look up her name in a history book.

ENSURING HISTORICAL CONSISTENCY

Thinking as you did at the time

The benefit of hindsight can alter how we tell a story. Neville Chamberlain has been treated harshly by history in proclaiming 'Peace for our time' . . . he was not so universally scorned on 30 September 1938.

The press has made us very familiar with the present royal family, but what were the feelings of the nation on 12 December 1936 when Edward VIII abdicated?

Trying to project your thinking back in time is not easy, but it makes for a great read.

Using the right words

A follow-on from the above point is trying to be as historically accurate as possible. This involves using the right words in the relevant periods of your life.

The list below will evoke different memories:

- wireless set (cat's whisker)
- radiogram
- radio
- record player
- stereo system
- hi-fi
- box brownie
- cine camera.

If you were lucky enough to get a television set for the coronation in 1953 you probably did not call it 'telly', 'TV' or 'the box'. And when did an aeroplane become an airplane or plane?

Taking care with time sequence

It is inevitable that your book will date ... indeed, it is likely to have dated since you first put pen to paper. If you write about your grandchildren, you will probably record their ages and maybe include their pictures. This is fine and is to be expected even though they might be a year older before the book makes its long-awaited appearance.

Where you can be careful is in the use of unspecific timescales. Words and phrases like 'ago' and 'last summer' will be ambiguous unless you link them to when you are writing or provide a date. To write, 'We visited Ralph in Spain two years ago' will be needlessly confusing. The reader will have to refer to the date when the book was written to work out when you mean. It is simpler for the reader if you write, 'We visited Ralph in Spain in 1998,' or, 'We visited Ralph in Spain two years ago, in 1998.'

TELLING THE STORY

Setting the context
All good stories need context. Take for example your first school:

- What was it called?
- Where was it?
- What was its size:
  - number of classes?
  - number of teachers?
  - the age range per class?
  - how many children per class?
- Is it still a school – or has it perhaps been converted to a two-bed-roomed house (that really shows its size)?
- How far away was it?
- How did you get there?
- Who took you to school?
- Who was the headmaster?
- Who was your teacher?
- What did he/she look like?
- How strict was he/she?
- Who was your best friend?
- Did you stay in touch?
- What forms of punishment were used?
- Were you ever on the receiving end?
- Why?
- If not, why not?
  etc.

All of these facts and hundreds more will be woven into the narrative to create the overall picture.

Utilising the why and the how
Many of the broad facts about our life will be similar to countless thousands of others. What differentiates us is how we interpret those facts – how we did what we did and our intentions behind those actions.

The fact that you went swimming every day of the summer holidays of 1936 is impressive, but what is more interesting is the inspiration behind it: the fact that you had seen Johnny Weissmuller as Tarzan earlier that year and you wanted to be able to swim like him. In fact, you also got into bodybuilding in a small way and started to watch what you ate. What was not so clever, though, was breaking your arm when you fell out of the tree trying to swing on the ivy . . . how was a 12-year-old to know that it wouldn't take such weight!

We can also apply these principles to others. Why did your parents live where they did and how did that come about? Think about their circumstances – you may arrive at some interesting conclusions.

Showing not telling

A significant tool used by the storyteller is to impart information by showing rather than telling. Describing the story of Dad hiding Granny's teeth is amusing, but it also shows us that he had a sense of humour and was a real tease. This is far better than writing, 'Dad had a great sense of humour.'

Including what you don't know

Often what you don't know can be of more interest than what you do, and is certainly worth including. If you don't know the answers say so. The fact that your school was in a poor area is of interest, but it is even more interesting to know that '. . . while it was in a poor area, we had no concept of rich or poor – we were all the same.'

Similarly, 'I never really thought too much about living through the war; we just carried on as best we could.'

DEVELOPING THE STORY

Creating interest from the start

Giving your book a strong opening will engage the reader's attention from the outset.

If you are starting the book at your birth, instead of writing, 'I was born . . .' try to think more laterally – perhaps something like this:

'I don't know if it was a ploy by my parents to fend off the seven-year itch, but I was born seven years after my elder brother Bob, 14 years into the marriage of my parents, Joe and Joyce Rice.'

As well as imparting a fair bit of information, you have also created some mystique.

Questioning your story

Your story will be obvious to you and you will therefore make many assumptions. Questioning some of these can lead to interesting results.

This is part of the benefit of attending a life writing class, or perhaps having someone to help you. By discussing the writing, it is easier to spot any ambiguities.

Such questioning is of particular importance when writing about growing up abroad or during the war – experiences that may well be far removed from your reader and which therefore need greater explanation.

CASE STUDY – Len takes to the air

Len was in meteorology during the war and one of his duties when based in Antigua was to observe weather conditions from the air. In his story he wrote, 'One day, when flying at 2,000 feet, I lost my glasses.'

Len had explained in an earlier chapter that he wore glasses from childhood, so this fact comes as no surprise. What does come as a surprise was that the aeroplane was of First World War issue and had an open cockpit. Without this information, the reason why he lost his glasses and the point of the anecdote is missed.

Embellishing a story

It is important to think through stories to ensure that a good anecdote is not overlooked. A story can often be embellished considerably simply by sifting it over in your mind.

The broad fact may be that you met Mary at a dance. But how did you hear about the dance? You may have seen it advertised in the corner shop when you popped in to buy some sweets because you missed the bus. You missed the bus because you had been chatting to Fred to find out the Test Match score. So, indirectly, the reason you met and later married Mary was because of cricket . . . and Mary hates cricket! This is a much better story than the bland fact of meeting Mary at a dance.

It is often when lying in bed that you will be able to develop stories in this way . . . but don't forget to have the notepad handy.

Q: How much artistic licence can I use?

A: You are the best judge of this.

Ultimately you don't want your book to be or sound false, but often you will find that the details are already there for a better story with a little thought.

Some people like to use speech in their writing – even when reporting a conversation at which it is obvious they could not have been present. This can be a useful device, but may come across as a little strange, certainly if overused. If in doubt, leave this for when you write your novel.

Further advice regarding speech appears in the next chapter.

ENGAGING THE READER

Helping the reader to empathise

Nothing warms a reader to the author more than shared emotions. We all feel them, and therefore empathise with the writer.

All emotions can be used, but if you feel uncomfortable with a 'Mills and Boon' love story, you might prefer to consider such feelings as embarrassment, frustration, shame and anger.

I still cringe when I think of the time I dropped a catch on the boundary in a house cricket match. I knew it was a six, and so did the third-formers on the boundary rope, but I swore blind it was only a four. It doesn't matter that Chris Parker won the game off the next delivery, and probably has never given it a second thought. I do and still feel embarrassed by the incident!

A book which lists only successes becomes a total bore and does not ring true. Everybody has some misgivings and failings. It's our flaws that are endearing.

Appealing to the senses

For those not born at the time, it is easy to think of the years before the 1960s as being grey and dull. They weren't . . . even though the records we have of that era may be in black and white. Despite the damp day and black and white television pictures, anyone could tell that there was nothing grey about Queen Salote of Tonga at Queen Elizabeth II's Coronation.

Try to recall colours, sounds, textures and smells. You might even be able to capture the bombardment of the taste buds when you tasted foreign food for the first time.

CASE STUDY – Monica remembers

Monica knew that she would need a little help in writing her life story. She heard that Sally helped in such projects and felt that sharing the experience would be fun.

At one of their monthly meetings, Sally asked Monica to describe the kitchen in the house in which she first lived. Monica amazed herself at what she recalled – the range, the copper and posser, the mangle and the skiffle board. She even burst into laughter when recalling the sticky flypapers on the ceiling -- after all, Monica later became a health inspector!

Something struck Sally about Monica's reference to the larder. She didn't spot it at first, but then it hit her – Monica sniffed each time she said the word 'larder'. Sally asked Monica to describe the larder. 'There was the slate, the milk jug covered with muslin edged with beads . . .' Then it came. Monica told Sally of the net bag hanging on the back of the larder door where her mother kept the meat. She added almost as an afterthought, 'Every time Mum opened the door she sniffed to check that the meat had not gone off.'

Without being aware of it, Monica's sniffing was mimicking her mother's actions all those years ago.

CHECKLIST

- Do you feel comfortable with how you want to come across in the book?

- How much of your life are you prepared to share with your readers?

ASSIGNMENTS

- Think of how you might start your book.

- Over the next few days try to embellish this in your mind.

- Think of the key stories in your life that might warrant similar development.

7

Some Writing Tools

BEING AWARE OF WRITING TECHNIQUES

The following techniques are often employed by writers. Please feel free to use or discard them as appropriate to the sort of project you have in mind.

Using flashbacks

When writing a chronological life story it can be difficult to deal with everything in order. For example, you may want to include something about your spouse's early life before you met. This is where flashbacks are particularly useful, but it is important to let the reader know what you are doing.

You might want to write something like:

'Before I continue with our married life together, I am going to take a step back to introduce Susan's family and relate something of her early life before we met.'

It will be obvious when the story gets back to the point where you left off. It is then simply a matter of continuing from there.

Using flashbacks for dramatic effect

Flashbacks can also be used to ensure that you don't give the story away too early, thereby losing any potential dramatic effect: 'Everything now all fell into place. I suddenly realised why Bill had been so keen to ensure I brought the camera along . . .'

Be careful, though. If flashbacks are used too often they lose their effect and the book can become confusing, not least in knowing what tense to use. If in doubt, keep it simple.

Introducing turning points

In writing a conventional chronological life story, there is little difference between a turning point and a decision. The fact that you were bored with studying and decided to get a job is both a decision and a turning point.

However, if you decide not to write exhaustively about a certain period of your life, your early years for example, the use of turning points can be very effective: 'There were three major turning points in my early life . . .'

Turning points are also useful if you include a reflective chapter at the end of your book: 'Looking back I can see that there were five major turning points in my life . . .'

Employing cliffhangers

Cliffhangers were regularly used by writers like Dickens whose work appeared in serial form and who needed to keep the reader gripped enough to buy the next issue. Of course, the device is employed by all writers of soaps, and from Saturday morning cinema-going days, many readers will be familiar with 'to be continued . . .'

Cliffhangers do not tend to feature significantly in autobiographies. If one does appear at the end of a chapter, the reader simply turns the page to find out more. Greater scope is provided when the cliffhanger is allied with the flashback:

'. . . so Dick and I married and moved into our idyllic new house, or so we thought. Little did we know what lay around the corner. But before I relate these nightmarish months, I would just like to record something of Dick's early life.'

Creating suspense

Again, with most life stories, there is little scope for high tension, but where there is it is best not to give the game away too early and spoil any potential impact: '. . . the lady who was to become my wife, give me four wonderful children and with whom I would share 34 blissful years until her untimely death in 1983.' Why bother writing anything more!

The fact that you found a half-brother in later life may be known to most people who will be reading your book, but perhaps not everyone. Learning about the existence of Alf after all those years when you had believed you were an only child came as a tremendous shock to you – why shouldn't it be so for others too? With hindsight, you can appreciate the clues that your mother dropped occasionally, but at the time you thought nothing of them. You might similarly want to drop the occasional ambiguity as readers also like to spot connections.

CASE STUDY – Dorothy writes
Having written about her childhood and parents, Dorothy moved on to Chapter 3 of her book:

> One day in late spring, when I was 7, Mum took me to one side and told me that I would be going on a journey. It was to be a temporary arrangement while she and Dad settled in America. I was not too worried; to me it was going to be a holiday. A gentleman, Mr Jackson, turned up to drive me to my new home where there were lots of other children.
>
> After a few months, Mr Jackson returned. I thought my time had come to go to America, but no, it was not to be. I didn't understand. I asked Mr Jackson why Mum and Dad couldn't take me. Abruptly he told me that my 'Mum' and 'Dad' had only ever been foster parents and that I was an orphan with no relations.
>
> I was devastated. I had had no knowledge of this.

Had Dorothy written: 'Until the age of 7 I was brought up by foster parents who then emigrated to America . . .' the impact of her story would have been lost. By writing in this way we can share a little of what Dorothy must have felt at the age of 7.

ADDING DEPTH TO THE STORY

Developing characters

The development of themes can also apply to people. Close friends and family, particularly parents and siblings, are likely to reappear in different chapters throughout your book. Rather than writing everything you know about them when they are first introduced to the story, you might like to develop their characters gradually as the story proceeds. A small anecdote here and an observation there will help the reader to get to know the person better as the writing unfolds, just as you did throughout your life.

Using speech

Speech is perfectly permissible in an autobiography, although overuse can reduce its impact. By reporting speech you have the opportunity of giving depth to the person concerned. To do this, though, the words must be realistic. For example, in speech, most people shorten words: 'do not' becomes 'don't'.

Similarly, speech has to be in character. Someone brimming with anger at having his car boxed in is unlikely to say, 'Excuse me, sir. I would be most grateful if you would be kind enough to move your motor vehicle.'

Embroidering themes within the book

Certain topics, like holidays and hobbies, may well crop up often in your story. For example, if you have been involved in amateur dramatics since childhood you have the choice of writing about it in a single chapter or weaving it throughout your story. The latter is usually preferable as it will include people relevant to different parts of your life. Of course, there's nothing to stop you writing a chapter entitled 'On the Boards' as well as including further references throughout the book.

KNOWING HOW TO USE CONFLICT

Using conflict points

Classically, conflict is defined in three ways:

- conflict with others
- conflict with nature
- conflict with self.

We tend to think of confrontation when we think of conflict, and often major confrontation at that. This doesn't have to be the case. The Chambers Oxford Dictionary describes conflict as 'to be incompatible'. In effect, it is any area when a decision has to be made. Chocolate or strawberry cheesecake for pudding could fall into this category!

Conflict with others
Best-selling blockbusters thrive on conflict points, and most books on writing encourage the use of this technique for dramatic effect ... and here they do mean serious confrontation. However, with books intended for a private audience it is advisable to play down potentially contentious areas rather than cause friction between friends or within families.

If you are feeling annoyed with someone, be careful what you write. While you are likely to be back on good terms again soon, grievances committed to print are there for posterity.

For writing of a potentially libellous nature, see Chapter 10.

Conflict with nature
This category covers all of nature, including the animal kingdom, so your childhood terrorisation by your neighbour's cat is included here.

Stories against nature, like the harsh winter of 1947, London smogs, and falling asleep in the sun and getting terrible sunburn, also feature if they are part of your experience.

Some such stories might have a humorous bent, others may be tragic. They are all part and parcel of life and are to be included.

Conflict with self
Here the opportunities are almost endless – you will be writing about conflict points without even thinking about them.

What might be interesting for you to consider in your book are the times when you struggled over a decision. You can explain how you arrived at your decision and, perhaps with hindsight, whether you feel you made the right choice.

CONSIDERING GRAMMAR

Writing for a sympathetic audience
Don't get too worked up about your grammar or spelling. This book is intended for a private, sympathetic audience. If you use 'who' instead of 'whom' are your readers really going to throw all your hard work down in disgust? If your grandfather had been guilty of such a heinous crime as a split infinitive would you discard his book in utter derision?

Those writing in longhand can expect assistance in both grammar and spelling if they have the manuscript typed. For those using a word processor, spell check and grammar check facilities will probably be available. However, be wary of computerised assistance with grammar as the script can become sanitised. Consider using the spell check, but ignore the grammar check and let your character shine through . . . even if there is the occasional split infinitive.

More help with grammar will be considered in Chapter 11 at the proofreading stage of the project.

Establishing your house style

All publishers have their own house style to ensure consistency within a book. This covers such areas as when to use upper case letters, numbering systems and punctuation. A few moments thinking about your own guidelines will similarly promote consistency and make for a better book.

The majority of decisions come down to your personal preference.

Using full stops

You were probably taught to use full stops in the following manner:

Dr. Blenkinsop O.B.E., D.F.C. was in the R.A.F.

The current trend is for minimal punctuation, therefore we see:

Dr Blenkinsop OBE, DFC was in the RAF.

Ultimately it does not matter which style you adopt, but sticking to one system will sit more comfortably with your readers.

Dealing with numbers

For consistency and to avoid writing, 'I collected seven thousand, six hundred and twenty-two pennies,' it is worth establishing a numbering system. For example, numbers between one and twelve can be written in words, thereafter digits are used. Exceptions to this are usually:

- dates (14th April)
- years (1962)
- money (£37.23)
- ages ('When I was 7 . . .').

Choosing quotation marks

Whether you use double or single inverted commas for speech is up to you. Again, make a decision and stick to it.

Providing emphasis

Some people are very liberal in their use of exclamation marks. Too many can grate and the usual advice is to use only one. If you are particularly flamboyant you may disagree, but please don't bombard your readers with too many!

Similarly, more than one question mark at a time is unnecessary, and any underlining should be used very sparingly, if at all.

Changing font

If your book is to be printed from a word processor, you will probably have the option of changing the style and size of font (lettering, print or typeface). To avoid too many inverted commas, you might consider a different or italicised font for:

- names of pubs – *The Ark*
- book titles – *Writing Your Life Story*
- songs – *The House of the Rising Sun*
- films – *Kind Hearts and Coronets*

CHECKLIST

- Does your story contain any natural moments of suspense?

- Are there any opportunities for employing flashbacks?

- How might conflict be used positively within your writing?

ASSIGNMENTS

- List the turning points in your life and think about how these might be included in your book.

- Write punctuation guidelines for your book.

8

Undertaking the Research

This chapter will give you an idea of how much research you might like to undertake before you put pen to paper. Some people will be happy simply to record what they remember; others will look to external resources and adopt a more exhaustive approach to their research. The choice is purely an individual one.

You might also like to read the next chapter which considers the process of writing before you return to this chapter and actively work through it.

Being selective

There are an amazing number of sources available to you. What follows is not exhaustive, but hopefully will give you a few ideas. While the emphasis here will be on your early life, the techniques are relevant for the whole project.

Before you go trekking round the country, it is worth looking around your own home. You'll be amazed at what you can remember without even going out of your front door.

Thankfully, the long-term memory appears to get better with age – remembering the name of our first school teacher is often easier than recalling what we had for lunch yesterday.

Prepare for the avalanche of memories!

MENTAL IMAGING

Thinking of your childhood home

With a pad of paper and pen to hand, try to picture your childhood home. If you moved house at the age of three or four you will probably want to picture your second home. Essentially, the focus should be on the residence that meant most to you in your early formative years.

Walking round the house

In your mind wander round the house trying to get your bearings and the general layout. If it helps, you might want to sketch a plan of the house noting down details, like who slept in which bedrooms and where the large pieces of furniture were situated.

Walk through the house and up the stairs. You might even remember odd things like the broken banister, how many stairs there were or the colour of that awful wallpaper. Think of the pictures on the walls, the light fittings and ceilings . . . sticky flypapers and a hole in the ceiling made from your catapult!

Going into the garden

Picture yourself standing in the garden. Was there an outside toilet . . . and where did Mum keep the mangle? This might even evoke the memory of your father's pre-Christmas custom of hanging a chicken by its feet in the mangle to drain the blood!

As memories come, jot down notes that you can later weave into stories.

CASE STUDY – Ron and June's research

Rather than trusting to memory, Ron decided to phone an estate agent in the town where he grew up. Ron had lived in a long road of 1920s houses and hoped that one might be up for sale. He was unlucky with the first call, but after explaining his quest, the estate agent was able to give him the telephone number of another agent who was selling such a property.

Ron was posted details of the house and with all the dimensions was able to draw an accurate plan. He was amazed how much smaller the house was than how he had remembered it.

June took her assignment a step further and wrote to the tenants at her old address. She received a very warm reply and was invited round for a cup of tea. June's father was a florist and the family of eight children lived above the shop. This had long since been converted into a house and the current owner was delighted to learn how it all pieced together. June spent a wonderfully nostalgic hour or two in her childhood home and now receives the occasional letter bearing her old address.

Refining the research

Try to think of events that took place in each of the rooms – breaking the sitting room window with a tennis ball when playing football in the garden with your brother ... it was his fault of course. Mum was particularly annoyed as there was a field the other side of the garden wall and so there was no excuse for playing ball games in the garden!

In your mind, spend time in each of the main rooms of the house: the kitchen, parlour and living rooms particularly.

CASE STUDY – George remembers

George shared a room with his older brother Robert. There were twin beds either side of a fireplace; this was never lit unless one of them was ill. George could remember nothing special about the room ... except. . .

Yes ... he remembered lying in bed at night and seeing the moon shining though the gaping curtains onto Robert's bed. George was curious. Why did the moon only ever shine on Robert's bed. One night George decided to ask his brother. Robert was 7.

Robert replied, 'The moon only shines on boys who are good.'

George was mortified. Why was only Robert good and not George as well?

A few nights later George woke in the middle of the night ... the moon was shining on him. God was saying that George was good.

So special was this memory to George that it was still with him over seventy years later.

Picturing furniture

Even some individual pieces of furniture may reveal a few anecdotes. If only that big old wooden kitchen table covered with the wax cloth could tell a story:

- We ate all our meals round it (no sitting with a tray on our lap watching TV ... there was no TV anyway).
- We did our homework on it ... sometimes.
- It was Mum's sewing table for 'make do and mend'.
- Bill had his head stitched on it.
- Dad plucked the chicken on it at Christmas.

- Scamp saw out his last hours on it before the vet arrived.
- Mum used it for making jam and Dad his homemade wine – Yuk.
- We even hid under it during the air raids.

Don't ignore any room – you might uncover a rare gem, like the anti-macassars on the armchairs in the front room that was only ever used on high days and holidays.

PAINTING CHARACTER PORTRAITS

The way you portray people in your writing will have a large impact on the readability of your book.

Significant people from childhood have helped to shape us and our characters. For example, traits from our parents will be recognisable in ourselves – both the admirable qualities and the frustrating ones! Readers of your book will also recognise those characteristics in you.

Defining the detail
Thinking about the following may help in describing key characters:

- What they looked like.
- What they usually wore . . . including the type of hat.
- Mannerisms – Dad's pipe and the nightly ritual in trying to light it.
- Their general disposition: happy, sad, jolly, always singing, whistling, nagging, clicking their fingers . . .
- What they liked doing to relax.
- Special sayings, like their first words on coming in from outside.
- Their habits.
- How they addressed you.
- How you addressed them.
  etc.

Sketching a brief family tree
Obviously, siblings, parents, grandparents and anyone else who might have lived with you will warrant special attention. To this end, sketching a brief family tree may ensure you don't forget any close relatives – for example, Uncle Jack who stayed with you for a few months after Aunt Maggie died.

Looking at old photos
Rifling through any photograph albums or old pictures stuffed in a shoe box will also stimulate the memory enormously.

These pictures will also remind you of the fashions of the day —
describe them.

Using anecdotes

Try to think of at least one anecdote about each of the main characters
from your childhood, about all characters if you can — even the postman
with his funny little habit of stopping his whistle mid-flow as he poked
the letters through the box, only to start up again from exactly the right
point as soon as the letters hit the mat . . . and the tune was always the
same — *The Lambeth Walk*.

RECALLING ROUTINES

Routines, particularly your mother's, probably dictated much of your
childhood existence. Such a routine might have been:

- Monday — wash day
- Tuesday — ironing
- Wednesday — cleaning the house upstairs
- Thursday — baking
- Friday — cleaning the house downstairs.

And there was always shopping to fit in. In the absence of a fridge this
may well have involved walking to the shops several times a week.

You might even be able to remember the meals associated with each
day's routine.

Then there were the different routines throughout the year:

- jam making
- potato clamping
- rearing day-old chicks
- storing eggs in isinglass
- making wine
- spring cleaning.

Remembering annual events

Annual events will also stimulate dozens of memories, particularly the
way you celebrated birthdays and Christmas. Remember, it is often the
smallest detail that is the most endearing.

There are likely to have been many other significant days in your
calendar:

- Easter
- Empire Day (24 May)
- May Day
- sports day
- end of school
- harvest festival
- Guy Fawkes night
- Christmas pantomime
- carol service.

There may also have been special annual events associated with your town or village:

- an inter-village football match
- church fete
- village fayre
- ox roast
- well dressing.

DESCRIBING THE NEIGHBOURHOOD

The neighbourhood where you lived as a child was probably your whole world for your first few years. Describing this will create wonderful pictures in the minds of your readers.

Consider walking your reader round the neighbourhood, introducing the main families as you proceed. Explain what sort of town or village it was, where most of the men worked and the type of shops. It might also be significant to note who owned cars in those days.

Then there were the various tradesmen:

- lamplighter
- coalman
- milkman
- the baker's boy
- the grocery boy
- muffin man
- knife sharpener
- Carter Paterson collection & delivery service
- organ grinder
- rag and bone man
- policeman.

Did any of the above have horse-drawn vehicles?

Descriptions of your environment will be all the more important if you lived abroad as a child where the wealth of customs will warrant special attention.

Tapping into the senses

What were the main sounds of your childhood? The siren and the all-clear klaxon during the war . . . there were certainly no church bells during the war years as they were only for warning of an invasion. Perhaps other sounds might be associated with the street traders. Was music a feature of your childhood?

Colours were also significant:

- Zebo black lead for the kitchen range
- the donkey stone for the front doorstep
- the smuts from the fireplace
- steam engines spoiling pristine white shirts
- the dull yellow sulphur of the smog.

Smells will also produce memories:

- moth balls
- disinfectants
- Sunlight soap in a solid block
- the gazunder!

Continuing the process

Even these few short pages have probably sent your mind spinning back many years. You can continue with the same techniques to encompass your school days, the church, youth club, etc.

LOOKING ROUND YOUR HOUSE

Your home is likely to be a treasure-trove of memorabilia. Dozens of stories will emerge as you look round each room:

- ornaments bought on holiday or given by special friends long since gone
- messages in the front of books kept since childhood
- your father's fob watch presented to him after 25 years at the bank.

The attic should not be forgotten either – this is where some of the best material may be found ... old school reports, 78 rpm gramophone records, etc.

You might want to take some of the smaller items of memorabilia to your special writing area. Certain photographs are likely to be required for the final production and you may want to store these together. As they will be out of circulation for some months, you may prefer to make notes referring to the photos in question rather than removing them from walls and shelves all over your home. If you are planning a surprise book, the absence of special photos in the house will be a give-away.

Including everything
Don't forget to take your note pad with you as you look at such things as:

- framed photographs
- pictures on the wall
- bric-à-brac
- books
- ornaments
- jewellery
- old greetings cards
- documents
- certificates
- school reports
- gramophone records
- old toys
- dried flowers
- your wedding dress.

You may also have an old family Bible containing a record of family names and important dates.

Let your imagination roam, and take your time ... you are likely to experience many different emotions.

ENLISTING THE HELP OF OTHERS

Reminiscing with friends
You might like to discuss particular ideas with friends or perhaps your partner. One thing will lead to another and, before you know it, a further chapter is in the making.

Asking elderly relatives

It may be that you have decided not to tell anyone about your book as you want it to be a surprise. However, even if that is the case, it still may be worth having a chat with any older relatives who might be around. They are too valuable a source to ignore, and will undoubtedly be happy to keep your secret safe.

Such relatives may be able to tell you details you never knew about your parents and provide you with fantastic background information. The odds are that they should be writing their own life story!

CARRYING OUT WIDER RESEARCH

You may feel that you have enough information for your purposes already without undertaking any wider research. However, if you want greater stimulation, there is plenty at hand.

Making use of the library

You may have plenty of reference books at home, but the local library will offer many more tempting opportunities.

Q: Are there any books in particular that you would recommend?

A: There are many excellent reference books available. However, one stands head and shoulders above the rest, *Dorling Kindersley's Chronicle of the 20th Century*.

Featuring one month per page, this huge tome trawls through the twentieth century. As each page bears a date, you can work out how old you were and place events accurately within your story. The book also contains many pictures, and in addition to reminding you of all major world events, you can see who won Wimbledon, changes in fashion and relive the hit songs and films of the year.

At £40 it is not cheap, but if you only buy one book, this is it.

Watching videos and films

Videos can provide a wealth of information, especially those that focus on a particular year. It might be worth watching the videos of some of the key years in your life to help get into the mood and to remind you of the social history.

Remembering the big films of that era will also help. You might recall where you first saw Disney's *Snow White* or *Gone with the Wind* and who you went with.

Listening to music and nostalgic tapes

Whether your idol was Frank Sinatra, Deanna Durbin or Bill Haley, certain songs will undoubtedly evoke particular memories.

Nostalgia tapes are also available of such classics as *Round the Horne*, *The Goons* and *Dick Barton, Special Agent*. Memories will pour forth when listening to these, and they may also have been the catalyst for in-jokes and family sayings. Alternatively they may have been the cause of family conflict if you were not allowed to listen to such programmes as *Valentine Dyall – The Man in Black*, yet your school friends were!

Reading specialist magazines

There are many nostalgia magazines available:

- *Yours*
- *Evergreen*
- *Best of British*
- *Goodtimes*
- *Saga*
  etc.

Service magazines might also be of help, as well as specialist organisations like *The Overseas Pensioner Association* for those who worked abroad.

Visiting museums

There are dozens of fabulous nostalgia museums that will send your memory reeling back to your childhood. Your nearest tourist information office and library will provide details of those in your area.

For those who want a trip to Gloucester, The Robert Opie Museum of Marketing and Packaging will not disappoint. You will see the packaging of hundreds of products from your childhood:

- *Reckitt's blue*
- *Robin Starch*
- *Strand cigarettes*
- *Beechams pills*
- *cod liver oil*

. . . the list is endless.

St Fagan's near Cardiff is also worth a visit. Its row of cottages furnished in different periods throughout the twentieth century is particularly fascinating. Beamish Open Air Museum in County Durham and Bethnal Green Museum of Childhood are also excellent.

There are war museums like the Cabinet War Rooms, the Imperial War Museum, Bletchley Park, etc., as well as dozens of aviation, naval and army museums.

Taking that extra step
The above list should provide ample scope for most people, but those looking for specialist information can refer to local and national records offices.

Another source worthy of consideration for the more enthusiastic researcher is the National Newspaper Library in Colindale, London N11. Here you can read through local and national newspapers from decades ago. It is a fascinating place, but worth booking first.

INCORPORATING SOCIAL HISTORY

Weaving in the detail
It is important to try to encapsulate your childhood for grandchildren who have never known anything but colour TV, trainers, mobile phones, fast food restaurants and computers.

Some events will be included because of their significance in your life, like the war, rationing and going to an Adam Faith concert. Other details will be added for social background, like your encounter with American GIs who were 'overpaid, oversexed and over here'!

Tying in important dates
Certain events in history are momentous and we can picture where we were when we heard the news. Depending on your age, events that you might want to consider include:

- the outbreak of the Second World War
- VE Day and VJ Day
- the death of King George VI
- the Coronation of Queen Elizabeth II
- Roger Bannister breaking the four-minute mile
- John F. Kennedy being shot
- Winston Churchill's death and funeral
- man landing on the moon.

CONSIDERING MORE IDEAS

For those still not satisfied that they have enough information, here are a few more ideas you might like to ponder:

- Why I was given my name . . .
- Stories I know about my birth . . .
- A day in the life of my mum; A day in the life of my dad (at the weekend maybe) . . .
- A typical week in my childhood . . .
- The importance of religion in my childhood . . .
- Childhood illnesses . . .
- Hospital visits as a child . . .
    - stitches . . .
    - something stuck up my nose . . .
- Things I broke:
    - my Mum's favourite vase . . .
    - my leg . . .
    - my brother's leg . . .
    - my heart when Granny died . . .
- The street traders of my childhood . . .
- My favourite toy . . .
- Family jokes; Family sayings; Family traditions . . .
- My first taste of foreign food . . .
- My first trip to London . . .
- Why I was caned; Why I was not caned . . .
- My favourite teacher . . .
- My best sporting moment; My worst sporting moment . . .
- The five things which have given me the greatest satisfaction . . .
- My proudest moment when I was 10 (or thereabouts); My proudest moment in my teens . . .
- When I felt most:
    frightened . . .
    elated . . .
    triumphant . . .
    content . . .
    ridiculous . . .
    embarrassed . . .
- What I most regret . . .
- The day my world fell apart . . .
- The five people I have known who I most admired . . .
- Different houses in which I've lived . . .

- The jobs I've had . . .
- Countries I have visited . . .
- My ten most memorable holidays . . .
- Pets we have had . . .
- I remember seeing my first:
    - hair dryer . . .
    - refrigerator . . .
    - radiator . . .
    - electric cooker . . .
    - television set . . .
- I remember first travelling:
    - in a car . . .
    - in a train . . .
    - in an aeroplane . . .
- Five 'what ifs' in my life . . .
- My ten best decisions; My ten worst decisions . . .
- Opportunities – taken and not taken . . .
    etc.

CHECKLIST

- Who were the important people in your childhood?

- How much social history do you want to include?

- Who might be able to help you in reminiscing?

- What wider research do you want to undertake?

ASSIGNMENTS

- Decide which day trips you might like to go on.

- Research which magazines might be useful.

- In the light of this chapter and the final list of ideas, review what insights you wish to share with your readers.

9

Ready to Write

Having planned the structure of your book, considered various writing techniques and looked at dozens of research ideas, you are now almost ready to start writing.

All that remains to do is:

- Decide the chapter where you want to begin writing.
- Review the chapter plan.
- Immerse yourself in memories.
- Revise the chapter plan.
- Get writing!

DECIDING WHERE TO START WRITING

By now you will have given some thought to where you want your book to begin. For most people this will be with what they know of their immediate forebears, or with their own childhood.

Just because the book might start with childhood, it does not follow that you have to write this chapter first. If you had a difficult childhood, for example, you may prefer to write about something else initially – maybe your first job or a holiday. You can always come back to your childhood once you are into the flow of writing.

The most difficult part of the process is putting pen to paper, so it is important that you begin your writing wherever you feel comfortable.

For convenience here it shall be assumed that the book begins at childhood.

REVIEWING THE CHAPTER PLAN

In Chapter 4 we looked at the structure of the book, breaking it down into various chapter headings. The more thorough you were then, the easier the next step will be.

Select the chapter where you want to start writing and review what you wrote under that heading. The aim here is to think along similar lines as when you wrote those notes.

IMMERSING YOURSELF IN MEMORIES

Essentially, you want to become immersed in that period of your history about which you are writing. All we are doing now is following the same techniques as before, but in greater detail.

In this you may be helped by:

- introducing year sheets
- familiarising yourself with the history of the period
- being prepared for the avalanche of memories.

Introducing year sheets

Time lines were considered when structuring the book. Year sheets follow the same principle but provide greater detail.

Assuming that you were born in 1930 and that you are focusing on your childhood, you would entitle sheets with the years from 1930 to 1945, one year per sheet. It helps to write how old you were alongside the year. By having separate sheets you can add any extra when necessary.

Dates worth recording might be when you started or changed schools. In this particular example the war will obviously feature as well. Of course, the two subjects will merge. Your twelfth birthday might be memorable because your party was celebrated in the Anderson shelter . . . and it was a very small birthday cake thanks to rationing!

Write down any memories relating to each year. It will be difficult to be precise, particularly in the first few years, but try to include any interesting anecdotes relating to that general period in your life.

Dealing with overlaps

Such an extensive period is likely to cover several chapters:

- childhood
- school days
- evacuation
- the war years.

This is inevitable with the early years where much of the information interlinks. While some topics will overlap chapters, it should be fairly logical where most stories belong.

Coloured highlighter pens are useful to link notes on your year sheets with the different chapters.

Familiarising yourself with history

A brief review of the period of history about which you are writing will open up many more ideas. It will also help you to be more specific about where anecdotes fit with the time sheets.

Social history is particularly important in these early chapters, but where your early years coincide with world events (like the Second World War), you will also want to weave them into your story. What you witnessed of such events will be of particular interest, maybe watching a dogfight or being frightened by a doodlebug.

Coping with the avalanche of ideas

As before, organisation is vital. All sorts of random recollections will come to you and it is important that none are lost, so have plenty of paper to hand, not just for the chapter in question, but for others as well.

REVISING THE CHAPTER PLAN

You are likely to have pages full of random memories. You can now connect all the similar ideas and rewrite them in some semblance of order. This is very much like the process undertaken in structuring the book.

Much of the information on different year sheets will be related and you will want to group these subjects together rather than write rigidly in years.

If you have masses of information you can divide the chapter. That's fine, but don't worry unduly – the chapter can always be divided at the review stage if you feel uncomfortable with it at that time.

Allowing thinking time

The subconscious is amazing. Once you delve back in time all sorts of memories will flash into your mind, often when you are least expecting them. Allow time to sift and develop ideas.

Settling on your chapter plan

Sooner or later, maybe after many revisions, you will be happy with your chapter plan. This will provide you with a sequence of the subjects to be covered and in which order.

SITTING DOWN TO WRITE

By the time you sit down to write you should be in the following position:

- have a planned structure for your book
- know at what point you want to start your writing
- have a detailed chapter plan
- feel comfortable with the amount of research you have undertaken
- have given special thought to the opening.

Keeping it simple

All you are trying to do is communicate your story. You speak fluently without deliberating over every word – write in the same uncomplicated way.

Try to keep your writing simple, and don't be tempted to rush to the dictionary and thesaurus every few sentences. Use your own vocabulary and enjoy what you are doing – just like writing a letter to a friend.

Write several pages in one sitting and don't be tempted to reread every paragraph before moving on to the next. You want the writing to flow.

When you reread a section you will probably want to fine-tune it a little. However, don't be too critical at this stage – that comes when you revise the book. What you are looking to do here is get several pages under your belt to boost your confidence.

Allowing for deviation

Even while you are writing you are likely to think of other ideas. If the memories are about a topic not yet touched upon, simply jot notes on your chapter plan to develop later.

Additional recollections concerning a subject about which you have already written can be accommodated by inserting a page at the appropriate place, as discussed in Chapter 3.

Understanding the challenge of the early chapter

Having written the first chapter you are well into the project and nothing should stop you now. If your first chapter is about your childhood you can be doubly pleased – it tends to be one of the more complex because of all the different subjects to introduce. Later chapters usually flow chronologically with fewer topics competing for attention.

REVISING PROVISIONAL TARGETS

Having written one chapter you will have a greater understanding of what is involved and how you work.

If the timescale for the project is an important consideration you might want to revise it. An unrealistic schedule might lead to disillusionment. It is better that you feel comfortable in undertaking a more modest project, or extend the anticipated timescale, rather than give up in frustration.

This is meant to be an enjoyable hobby. It is therefore important that you don't put yourself under too much pressure and resent ever having begun.

CONTINUING THE PROCESS

Keep on writing

Essentially all you need do now is follow the same steps as before. It's that simple!

Invariably when writing some of the later chapters you will think of additional memories for inclusion earlier in the manuscript. Tying these memories into the relevant chapter is satisfying as it makes for a more thorough book. This process is likely to continue right up to the time the book is bound . . . and even then you will think of things you have forgotten!

Q: I seem to be writing a great deal about my early life. Is it too detailed? I know I won't have so much material later.

A: Most books tend to be weighted in favour of the early years. Maybe three-quarters of your writing will cover the first 30 years or so. This is not unusual – after all, this period of your life involves more scene-setting. These years will also be of greater interest to your children as they contrast your childhood with life today.

DEALING WITH WRITER'S BLOCK

Hopefully you will enjoy your writing. However, even if you are highly motivated there may come a time when the words do not flow so easily. If you find yourself in that position, here are some techniques you might like to consider.

Being disciplined

Most writers agree that there is no substitute for discipline. When their livelihood depends on what they produce they just have to persevere. Thankfully, you are not in such a position. This project is intended to be enjoyable and it is hoped that some of the following methods will be more appealing.

Creating routines

Some people are most inspired at a certain time of day. Alternatively, there might be a day of the week when everyone is out and you know you won't be disturbed. If you recognise such patterns, use them to your advantage.

Setting realistic targets

If you are feeling a little daunted by the size of the project ahead, make sure that you focus only on smaller tasks like topics within individual chapters.

Don't set yourself too great a target like writing for five hours at a stretch. Even twenty minutes can be very productive and might help you through a difficult patch. You may then feel inspired to spend longer next time.

Leaving off in mid-flow

It is good to leave a session of writing wanting to write more. In recognition of this, some writers even stop a paragraph or sentence in mid-flow so they can pick it up next time.

If you don't like this approach, you may at least want to leave a stimulating topic to start with at the next session.

Reading

Rereading what you wrote last time is an excellent way of getting back into your stride. Alternatively, you might want to review your chapter plan.

If inspiration is still not coming, you can try reading the introduction explaining why you wanted to write in the first place.

Reading another autobiography can also be helpful in triggering ideas . . . as long as you don't become too engrossed and spend the whole afternoon on that book!

Being constructive

If you don't feel like writing, you can use your time constructively in
other ways:

- reviewing the book structure
- revising the chapter plan
- brainstorming another chapter
- reading history or reference books
- doing some other research
- thinking
- planning the book launch!

Imposing a deadline

If all else fails, you might want to impose some deadlines on yourself.
This is particularly effective when you make a commitment to someone
else. If you tell a friend that you would like to send a chapter at the end
of the month for review you will feel a responsibility to get the chapter
written.

A writing circle or external writing partner fulfils a similar discipline
for those who never completed their homework until the night before it
had to be handed in!

CASE STUDY – Shirley's SFNs

Shirley was enjoying writing her life story, but she found it
difficult to get started. Sitting down at the typewriter was no problem, but getting into the flow was not so easy until Shirley devel-
oped her own special technique.

Before continuing with her life story, whenever Shirley sat
down to write she typed two or three paragraphs about the few
days since her last session. She might include frustrations with the
washing machine repairman or the wonders of modern super-
markets. Whatever it was, it got Shirley into a writing frame of
mind and she then found it easy to turn her attention to her 'real
writing'.

Although obviously not included within the book, 'Shirley's
famous notes' as they became known, formed a fascinating record
in their own right. Incidentally, since completing her book Shirley
has started a diary.

CHECKLIST

● Where do you want to start writing?

● Are you fully prepared?

● How might you deal with writer's block?

ASSIGNMENTS

● Prepare a chapter plan for your first chapter.

● Write your first chapter.

● Revise any provisional targets you set for writing your life story.

10

Difficult Areas

You might encounter some difficulties in writing your life story. This chapter will help deal with such areas.

Ultimately, this is your book . . . only write what you feel comfortable about.

THINKING ABOUT YOURSELF

Being emotionally prepared

A vast array of memories will flood forth as you reflect over your life. While this is likely to be a hugely enjoyable process, you may also encounter some painful emotions. When you know that you are coming to such a stage in your story, allow yourself the space you need to be emotionally prepared.

The death of a loved one may well fall into this category. Writing can be cathartic, and you will also have the opportunity to pay tribute to this special person in your book, but it is worth being prepared before you open up any painful memories.

Allowing a passage of time

Writing about the war can similarly produce powerful emotions and it sometimes takes 30, 40, 50 years or more before these memories can be reviewed. Some people find that they can never write about such times.

If you decide to include painful memories you might be deflected in your desire to finish the rest of your story. It is therefore advisable to have an easier chapter lined up to get back into the flow after you have written about a traumatic event.

CASE STUDY – David's honesty

David was progressing well with his writing, but there was a period looming that he did not know how to handle. It covered five years in his life when things were difficult, both with his career and domestically. He did not want to hurt his wife or children by what he wrote.

David had the choice of fudging over these five years – after all, there was no need to describe them in detail, and with a bit of creative wording he knew that most readers would be none the wiser. However, David wanted to acknowledge that he'd had problems without going into any details – he didn't know how much he'd be able to remember anyway.

In the end, David wrote the following: 'I found the next five years of my life very difficult. I don't know if I cannot or do not want to remember them, but I am moving on in my story to . . .'

DECIDING WHAT TO INCLUDE

Knowing who to mention

Most of the people to be mentioned in your book will have been highlighted in the various chapter plans, but it is worth ensuring that significant people have not been omitted.

Those likely to be reading your book
You probably feel that you can name all those who will be reading your book – the list may be longer than you envisage. Once people hear that you have written a book, you will be surprised who might ask to borrow a copy: neighbours, friends from the bowls club or church, old work colleagues, etc.

You might like to include something along the lines of:

'For the last few years Betty and I have been members of the local social club. Jean and John, Fred and Jill, Max, Bob and Wilf have all been good friends and we look forward to our monthly get-togethers.'

They will be delighted to be included in your book, and it may well save you a little embarrassment when they ask to borrow a copy.

The Christmas card list is also likely to reveal both names and anecdotes for inclusion in your book.

Writing about the family

If you have children, knowing how much to include about them will partly depend on the intended audience for your book. As a general rule, it is reasonable to include a few anecdotes about them until they left home, thereafter you will probably just cover the main events in their life: career, marriage, house moves and any grandchildren. This follows the assumption that the book is about your life not theirs, and that if they want to write their own book in future years, that is their prerogative.

Being even-handed

For the sake of family harmony, it is important to be even-handed when mentioning any children and grandchildren. There may be more to write about the oldest grandchild, but the others warrant their share of attention. While favouritism is not intended, it can be perceived.

Using in-jokes

In-jokes are fine – after all this is a family book. Some family jokes will go over the heads of many readers. That is acceptable if the reference is not obvious. Where the reference is obvious, you may have to explain the point so that others can also share the fun.

DECIDING WHAT NOT TO INCLUDE

Dealing with libel

Libel is defined as writing something that will damage a person's reputation or their livelihood. Even if you know what you write is true, you have to be able to prove it. Any court proceedings are likely to be emotionally traumatic and financially ruinous.

Even changing the name of the person will not get you off the hook if they can reasonably be identified by your writing.

The simple advice here is to steer clear of anything that is libellous or potentially libellous. If you feel that badly towards someone, why even give them the satisfaction of a mention in your book?

If it is a subject of great importance to you, at least try to be balanced and present the other point of view – even if you do not agree with it. Remember, if you write anything vitriolic, it is likely to say more about you than the other person!

Handling relationships

You need to be diplomatic if writing about past relationships.

Writing about divorce

If writing about your own divorce, the safe option is to say little. There will be your ex-partner, as well as perhaps a current partner and any children to consider – nothing will be achieved by putting anything hurtful in print.

If the divorce relates to another couple, maybe involving a child or sibling, question why the information needs to be included. If it does, avoid detail and consider checking your provisional writing with the parties concerned.

Writing about old flames

Again, if the subject is likely to be contentious, think twice. Ask yourself what is to be gained by including the information and who might find it difficult to read. Your partner may find it insensitive if you write in detail about old flames. If you decide to proceed, it might be worth seeking your partner's approval over the wording before it appears in the final book.

Relationships that are further afield, maybe concerning children, have less of a part in your book. If they want to write about them in future years that is up to them. If they are happy for you to include details, be sensitive.

CASE STUDY – Helen writes creatively

Helen had got to the stage in her story when she was going to write about her daughter, Jane. On leaving university, Jane went to work in France where she shared a flat with her boyfriend, Steve. Helen wrote, 'When Jane got the opportunity to go to France, she needed no second invitation. Once in Lyon, Jane began to teach English at a language school, sharing a small apartment with her boyfriend, Steve.'

Helen asked her daughter about this wording; Jane was happy with it, even though she is now married to Paul and they have four children. Helen still felt a little uncomfortable and in the end wrote, 'Once in Lyon, Jane began to teach English at a language school, sharing a small apartment with a friend.' Helen felt that if Jane wanted to write her own book in years to come and mention Steve, that was up to her.

Getting things off your chest

Words said in jest down the pub might not look quite so funny when printed in a book. Just because you have written something does not mean that it has to appear in the final presentation. The very process of writing may have served the purpose of getting it off your chest.

Dealing with sex and colourful language

While blockbusters may be sprinkled liberally with sex and colourful language autobiographies intended for friends and family rarely fall into the same category.

You know your own audience, but the general advice here is to be careful not to offend loved ones.

GETTING THE FACTS RIGHT

Remembering major historical dates

Most dates can be easily checked in reference books. If you can't find a precise date, the month and year, or just the year, will suffice. If you get the date wrong, someone might notice, but it is not going to cause offence.

Remembering significant family dates

The dates of birthdays and anniversaries are likely to be of greater importance than national milestones – at least, the consequences of getting them wrong will be more significant! If you put the wrong date for your grandson's birthday, you are likely to hear about it . . . if not from him then from his parents. It really is worth checking these facts thoroughly. The last thing you want to do is cause offence.

Checking the spelling of names

The same holds true for names as it does for dates. If Rachmaninov is spelt 'Rachmaninof' you are unlikely to face many repercussions. Spelling a grandchild's name incorrectly is a different matter. Again, check thoroughly.

ENDING THE BOOK

Knowing where to finish

If you set out with the intention of writing about a certain period of your life, the ending of the book will be obvious: when you were demobbed or when you retired maybe.

Using a milestone

In writing a full autobiography it is likely that you will want to bring the narrative up to date. Rather than let the writing trail off, you might find it easier to close at an appropriate milestone. This might be:

- your 64th birthday
- completing your year as captain at the bowls club
- your 47th wedding anniversary
- the birth of your latest grandchild or great niece
- the Millennium, or the new year of 2001 . . . 2002 . . .
- the cruise to Madeira
- a reunion.

Finishing positively

Readers like to feel uplifted at the end of a book. You might want to consider looking to the future . . . 'As this book draws to a close I look forward to catching up with all my other hobbies and, who knows, in 15 years' time I may have to consider a sequel!'

Bringing a smile to the face of the reader

If it is your style, you might consider ending on a humorous note. One author concluded his magnum opus with the imaginary scene of reading his book to his grandson:

'That's enough. We close the book now and you must go to sleep and dream.'
'Goodnight, Granddad.'
'Goodnight.'
'Oh, Granddad?'
'Yes?'
'Granddad, will you leave your book?'
With pride swelling in my chest I leave the book on Tom's bedside table.
'Thanks Granddad.'
'Do you want to read it in the morning?' I ask.
'No. But if I stand on it, I can reach the top of the cupboard.'

Writing a summary

Having completed their manuscript, some people like to review their life, reflecting on the changes they have witnessed and the people they have met.

CHECKLIST

- What areas of your life do you not want to share?

- Is there anything in your book which is potentially libellous?

- Is anyone likely to be offended by what you include? If so, does it need to be in your book?

ASSIGNMENTS

- Write a list of the people who might conceivably read your book.

- Check important family dates and the spelling of names.

- Consider how you might end your writing.

11

Revising the Manuscript

A few hours spent in revising your manuscript will reap rewards disproportionate to the effort expended. We all make mistakes, but the majority of these can be corrected with a thorough review.

In revising your manuscript there are three main areas to consider:

- the structure and style
- the content
- the grammar.

You should be able to consider all of the above areas in one reading, especially if an independent proofreading is being considered – more of which later in the chapter.

Taking a break

Once you have written your manuscript it is worth taking a break to allow a certain distance and objectivity for when you review your writing. Having just completed the book your mind is likely to be too cluttered to be able to look at the overall structure in a detached manner.

If you feel that getting out of the habit of working on your book will be counter-productive, you can always spend the time sorting any photographs to be included or perhaps planning how the book is to be launched.

REVISING THE STRUCTURE AND STYLE

The idea of this part of the review is to ensure that the manuscript is well structured and that the story flows smoothly.

Starting with the introduction

In reading the introduction you will remind yourself of the purpose for writing the book and, perhaps, what you intended to include. If the final manuscript has deviated from these original intentions, or if there is anything else you would like to add as a result of writing, simply amend the introduction.

Reviewing the first chapter

The first chapter was probably written many months before the final one, during which time your style is likely to have changed. It sometimes takes a chapter or two to find your writing voice, something which sits more comfortably when the project is underway. Additionally, the early chapters often contain fewer insights as the author establishes how much detail should be included. As a result, some people choose to re-write, or at least elaborate upon, the first chapter.

Proceeding a chapter at a time

There is no ideal length for a chapter, but try not to make it too long. A useful rule of thumb is to read through a chapter in one sitting and see if it feels comfortable. It may be that you want to divide a chapter and can spot an appropriate place. Alternatively, you might want to join two or three short chapters together.

As chapters often have an introduction and a conclusion, any restructuring may result in having to refine a few sentences.

Finalising the chapter headings

Chapter headings are not essential, although they serve to tell the reader what lies ahead. Hopefully they are also of some assistance in the writing of the book, and the use of them is encouraged if you have no strong views to the contrary.

In life stories chapter headings usually run along the lines of:

- Meet the Family
- Early Years
- School Days.

These are perfectly adequate, although it is worth avoiding the overuse of words like 'years' – 'Early Years', 'School Years', 'War Years', etc. – unless you are deliberately seeking symmetry.

Thinking laterally about chapter headings

You can be more creative in your use of chapter headings if that is your style.

- a quotation
- something intriguing
- a verse from the Bible
- a stanza of your own poetry
- a song title
- some Latin.

Of course, you can also have a chapter heading followed by a quotation or verse as a sub-heading.

REVISING THE CONTENT

Identifying structural imbalance

Having taken a break you will be in a better position to look at the overall structure of the book. Any glaring imbalance should be obvious.

It may be that you decided to include your childhood diary in the first chapter of your book. You now appreciate that 27 pages was a little too long and this has created an imbalance in the book. Rather than discard such valuable information, consider including the diary as an appendix, perhaps keeping two or three pages in the first chapter.

The appendix can be a wonderful depository for any information that would otherwise create an imbalance in the book.

Looking for omissions

Having taken a break you will be in a better position to spot any omissions – a common problem when you are so familiar with the story.

For example, your brother Jeremy was obviously introduced in your childhood chapter, but you now notice that you made no reference to his wife Claire. And this is despite the fact that you were Jeremy's best man and the wedding was an unforgettable occasion!

Checking against a list of names

To ensure that you have not omitted any significant people, before you review the manuscript write an exhaustive list of names of those who should feature in your story. Particularly useful are:

- Christmas card lists
- photograph albums
- family tree
- lists of those likely to read the book.

As you read through the manuscript tick off the names as they are mentioned. If you have chatted to friends about your book, it is all too easy to think that you have recorded a story when in fact you have only talked about it.

Spotting duplications

As your writing will have been undertaken over a long period of time, it is not uncommon to find that you have written about the same event twice. If you review the whole manuscript in a relatively short period, such duplications should jump out at you.

Eliminating excessive material

On rereading your manuscript you may decide that some details are superfluous, that you got a bit too carried away. Only you can be the judge of this, but prune sparingly and avoid discarding any real treasures. As has been stated before, the fact that you remembered these details from maybe 50 or more years ago must mean something. What would you cut from your grandmother's book if you were given the choice?

Correcting continuity errors

It is worth being on guard for continuity errors. For example, if you mention your nephew before writing about your sister even meeting, let alone marrying, her husband, the reader may be justifiably confused.

CASE STUDY – Jack's fit of pique

Jack was feeling a bit fed up. He had intended to get down to his writing straight after lunch, but then Harry turned up and proceeded to tell him all about the problems on the allotment . . . it was not as if Jack had not heard them all a dozen times before.

It just so happened that Jack was up to the point in his story when he and Sheila went on holiday with Harry and Vera. As a bit of fun Jack related how Harry had been insulted by the bar tender for being so long-winded in ordering the drinks. Jack knew that it was a sore point with Harry, but what was the harm – Harry didn't even know about the book?

In reviewing his manuscript a few months later, Jack decided to remove the reference about the bar tender. He was glad he did, because Harry later heard about the book via Vera and asked to read it.

Being diplomatic
A comment that sounded funny when first written might not appear quite as amusing once reviewed at a later date.

Finalising the title
If you have not settled on a title, the time is looming when you will have to make a decision. Hopefully, by now you will have a shortlist of ideas. Bouncing these around with a close friend may help to arrive at the final choice.

REVISING THE GRAMMAR

It is amazing how many simple mistakes can be found when reading through an entire manuscript, but take comfort from the fact that the more you spot the less are left for your readers to tease you about.

Remember to pay particular attention to names, especially family names, as well as dates of birth, etc.

Referring to your house style
Before you start reading through the manuscript review what you wrote for your house style. You might want to refine this, but once you settle on a style use that throughout the manuscript. Consistency in simple matters, like double or single quotation marks, will at least avoid frustrating the reader.

Looking for anything that jumps out
If words jump out at you they need changing. Similarly, if you stumble over a phase, simplify it. Your words should not draw the attention of the reader away from the story.

Avoiding too many helpful, interesting, clever adjectives
We can sometimes try too hard to be descriptive – perhaps a throwback to English lessons at school when the teacher wanted to assess the diversity of our vocabulary. There is no such test here; too many adjectives can be annoying and the implication is that you are trying too hard. A well-chosen adjective is far more powerful than three or four bland ones.

Dealing with repetition
Sometimes repetition is used to provide emphasis: 'The house was huge, the garden was huge, the swimming pool was huge.' Unless you have deliberately sought to employ this technique, try using a different word.

Identifying favourite word syndrome

We all have favourite words which we overuse. If these jump out at you reduce their frequency. An independent proofreader will help identify these, and the word search facility on a word processor can also be helpful.

Clarifying ambiguities

If something sounds ambiguous to you, it is almost certain that the reader will be in the dark. Be particularly wary when using 'he' or 'she' when there are several people mentioned – don't forget, you know the story, your reader does not.

SEEKING ASSISTANCE

A fresh pair of eyes is always useful in proofreading – knowing what comes next makes it all too easy to miss our own mistakes.

Finding an independent proofreader

A friend or relative might be very happy to read your manuscript. If so, make it clear that you are looking for an objective review and that you will not be offended if they come back with dozens, or even hundreds, of queries. Friends can sometimes shy away from a vigorous review in an attempt not to offend.

To avoid any awkwardness, you might prefer to employ a professional proofreader – it is not as expensive a service as you might imagine. Sources can be found at the end of this book.

Independent proofreaders have the advantage over a friend or relative in that they do not know you and therefore cannot make certain assumptions. If they don't know who Fred is, they will say so. They are therefore more likely to pick up on any continuity and structural inconsistencies.

Opting for a collaborative review

If you are having your manuscript proofread, consider reviewing the manuscript together. Two minds are certainly better than one when it comes to revising a manuscript – the exercise is more thorough and great fun.

Reading aloud

If your assistant reads aloud you will hear your book as others will read it. In listening to the emphasis placed on the narrative, any clumsiness or ambiguity will jump out at you, resulting in the need to either rephrase a few words or alter the punctuation.

If you do opt for the collaborative approach, ensure that you can sit down together for a few hours at a time where you will not be disturbed. Also allow for the fact that your assistant is likely to ask questions about your story which will result in the need to elaborate on your writing in certain areas.

MAKING THE WORD PROCESSOR WORK FOR YOU

If you have either used a typewriter or written your life story in long-hand, it is likely that you will want it transcribed onto a word processor at some stage. This will give you greater choice for the production of your book, more of which will be discussed in the next chapter.

If you employ someone to do this for you, it is worth paying a little more for them to undertake some basic editing at the same time. However, ensure that you give clear guidelines as to how much initiative they can exercise – perhaps asking them to place a pencil mark alongside any passages they revise.

However good your typist/editor is, some alterations will be required when you review their work. In correcting your mistakes they are sure to introduce some of their own. Ensure that any alterations will be undertaken in a timely and cost-effective manner.

Using the spell check facility
The spell check facility is wonderful, but can lead to laziness when reviewing a manuscript. Most spell checks only pick out incorrectly spelt words, making it easy to overlook such common typing mistakes as 'our' instead of 'out'.

Using the grammar check facility
As mentioned earlier, over-dependence on the grammar check facility can diminish the character of a book. However, they are useful in checking the context of words. For example, it would highlight the 'our/out' problem defined above.

Attaining perfection
Unless you are a rare genius, forget the idea of perfection in a book of 50,000 or more words. Sadly, most books contain errors . . . maybe even this won. You can proofread your manuscript 83 times, and on the 84th reading still spot another mistake.

It is important to reduce the number of errors as much as possible, but family and friends love you for being you. If this is your audience, they won't mind if there is the odd glitch – it is inevitable.

CHECKLIST

- Is the style of your first chapter consistent with subsequent chapters?

- Are you happy with your chapter headings?

- Have you written the sort of book you intended?

ASSIGNMENTS

- Rewrite the introduction.

- Revise any writing you feel uncomfortable about before it's too late.

- Think of someone who can help you with proofreading and decide if you would like a collaborative approach.

12

Presentation

The purpose of this chapter is to provide options for the presentation of your book. First impressions are so important, and having worked hard on getting your manuscript right, it is worth spending time on the final presentation. Something well presented and pleasing to the eye will increase the reader's enjoyment immeasurably and also provide you with considerable satisfaction.

We shall be looking at the presentation of a single book at this stage. Ideas for binding and producing additional copies in a cost-effective manner will be considered in the final two chapters.

CHOOSING YOUR MEDIUM

Many of the principles for presentation are the same whether the manuscript is handwritten, or produced on a typewriter or a word processor. A book can be achieved via any of these, although more advanced forms of presentation, like changing the size of the font, will require a word processor.

Transcribing the manuscript

If you had intended to keep your manuscript in a handwritten format but have revised that decision, it is relatively cheap and easy to have it transcribed onto a word processor.

If the manuscript is to be word-processed:

- Agree a price by the number of words typed, not per hour. This ensures that the bill is not open to question and can be easily checked.

- Obtain quotations from at least two or three different sources as prices can vary considerably.

- Agree in advance how changes will be made. These will probably have to be charged per hour.

- In addition to receiving the manuscript on paper, ensure that you are also provided with the files on $3\frac{1}{2}$" disk. This way you have the option of going elsewhere for editing or further copies.

Suggestions for finding typing services can be found at the back of this book.

CONDUCTING SOME SIMPLE RESEARCH

Collect a dozen or more books from around your house and scrutinise them closely. Try to choose as many different styles as possible, including those containing pictures and other illustrations.

With a critical eye, now look at such attributes as:

- the size of the page
- the size and style of font
- spacing between lines
- margins
- the opening few pages
- the style of chapter headings and any other titles
- how pictures are presented and their associated captions
- any appendices.

Defining your own style

As a result of this research decide which presentations you like best and why. Don't limit your expectations – with modern production techniques plenty of options are available to you. For example, pictures do not have to appear in one block in the middle of the book but can be inserted at the appropriate place in the story.

It is often easier to spot what you do not like about the presentation of a particular book. Maybe the size of the writing is too small making it hard to read, or the pages come across as being heavy on the eye because of small margins.

Deciding on the size of the book

Q: What book dimensions do you recommend?

A: The dimension of the book will depend on how much you've written. Assuming this to be in excess of 30,000 words, a presentation up to A4 size is possible, although you may prefer something smaller.

A larger page provides greater flexibility: some pictures that would otherwise have to be reduced can appear at their actual size, and more pictures fit onto a page. All this helps to keep costs down.

If you are to have your final manuscript bound it will need to be trimmed a little, so bear this in mind when thinking about the size of the book.

PREPARING THE INTRODUCTORY PAGES

In the books you research, there will be a combination of most or all of the following:

- title page
- copyright
- dedication
- acknowledgements
- table of contents
- list of illustrations
- introduction/foreword/preface.

You might notice that some books always start new chapters on the right-hand page, even if the adjacent left-hand page is blank. If you adopt this convention, you might want to extend it to the introductory pages as well. The usual exception to this is the copyright, which is likely to appear on the reverse of the title page or dedication.

There is no fixed pattern for the sequence of the introductory pages, for example the acknowledgements might appear before or after the table of contents. Again, decide which structure you prefer.

Title page

This is simple enough. It merely states the title of the book, and perhaps a subtitle, along with your name. The important thing here is to ensure that the page is well presented as it is what the reader sees first in your book.

How your name appears is entirely up to you, and is dependent upon the audience for your book. Overleaf are a few suggestions:

- Dr W.L. Barton MBE, FRCPE
- Dr William Barton MBE
- Dr Bill Barton
- Bill Barton
- Grandpa

Copyright

Anything you write of an original nature becomes your copyright as soon as the ink hits the page. The same is also true of material produced on a word processor or dictated onto tape. There is not even any need to write 'Copyright Michael Oke 2001' . . . but it is rather satisfying to see it in print so you may as well indulge yourself after all your hard work!

Dedication

Books don't have to have a dedication, but it seems a shame to miss the opportunity, and inclusion will always be very special to those mentioned.

You might want to dedicate the book to the memory of a loved one, and/or opt for a catchall:

'This book is dedicated to my entire family, past, present and future, and especially to my wife Mychelle whose love and support is treasured.'

Acknowledgements

This section is used to give thanks to all those who have assisted in the writing of the book. If your son painstakingly typed your manuscript into the small hours of the morning on many occasions, it is at least worth thanking him. Similarly, an unpaid friend may have spent dozens of hours proofreading the manuscript . . . even though you might not have agreed with all the comments.

It is also worth thanking your partner for allowing you the space to write the book, for providing countless cups of tea, answering your telephone calls and giving encouragement when it was needed.

Some people also like to include, '. . . and to my parents, without whom none of this would have been possible.' You might not want to go this far, but you get the idea.

Table of contents

The convention is to begin listing the contents from the page after the table of contents. This will usually be the list of illustrations, or perhaps the introduction.

List of illustrations
This is not compulsory, but if you have included pictures it's a good idea to provide a listing ... if only to make it easier for the family to find pictures of themselves.

Introduction/Foreword/Preface
These terms are largely interchangeable – select whichever you prefer. You can have more than one, for example a foreword and an introduction, especially if someone else is making a contribution as with this book.

In an autobiography this section usually explains why you embarked on the project and for whom the book was written. You will have drafted most of this at the outset of the project, revising it towards the end. It should therefore be in pretty good shape by this time and will only require a few adjustments.

Something else for you to consider including in this section is a catchall to protect you against the grumblings of any pedantic readers:

> 'This book was written with the best of intentions, so please forgive any offence caused by what I have either included or omitted ... certainly none is intended.'

Including a picture of yourself
While you probably did not see this in any of the books you researched, a picture of the author is a pleasing touch at the front of a life story. A photo in your earlier years, maybe between 15 and 25, is even better, because you can end the book with an up-to-date picture to provide symmetry.

A picture at the beginning is best placed after the title page or the dedication.

DESIGNING THE BOOK

The measure of a well-presented book is how pleasing it is to the eye. However, as is often the case, creating something simple involves some complex considerations.

Creating the first impression
Our first impressions of a page are dictated by:

- the style of the font
- the size of the font

- the size of the margins
- the layout
- the quality of print.

Choosing the font

If your book is handwritten, the style and size of your writing will have been honed over many years. Your greatest consideration will be legibility – if your handwriting is poor, you must consider having the manuscript typed.

The more sophisticated typewriters, and all modern word processors and printers, will give you a selection of font styles and sizes. Experiment to see what looks best, perhaps also asking a few friends for their opinions.

Adjusting the margins

Small margins make the page look overloaded with text. Increasing the size of the margins can have a dramatic effect on the appearance. Again, it is worth experimenting.

If the book is to be bound, the edges will need to be guillotined. You will need to leave slightly larger margins to allow for this – one centimetre top and bottom and a slither on the right-hand edge should be sufficient.

While margins are still of consideration with the handwritten text, if lined paper is being used, the top, bottom and left-hand margins will be pre-set. Of greater importance here is the space between the lines. Again, experiment until you feel comfortable with the overall appearance.

Designing the page layout

Too many words on a page can leave the reader feeling daunted – plenty of space will improve the appearance of your book significantly. However, there are a few other considerations worth bearing in mind.

Dealing with speech

If you have decided to use speech within the book, this can be presented two ways:

- Within the run of the text:

    When Mary came into the room she exclaimed, 'Boys, what on earth do you think you're doing?' Ted, taken totally by surprise, stuttered, 'We we we we're, ju-just looking for my old photo album . . .'

- As scripted conversation:

    'What's for tea, Mum?' asked Jim.
    'Sausages,' came back the reply.
    'Great. Can Billy stay for tea? His mum says it's OK.'
    'Thanks for asking me first,' Mum quipped.

The decision rests with you, but where there are more than two or three exchanges, scripting the conversation is worth considering.

Presenting paragraphs
Again, there are two conventions to consider:

- indenting the first word of a new paragraph
- leaving a line between paragraphs, starting new ones on the left margin.

Either is fine, as long as you are consistent within the book.

Handling headings
Be careful to ensure that each chapter heading appears with the same spacing and font size and type.

Using section breaks
Sometimes within a chapter there is a change of subject. The use of a few asterisks will show the reader that you are moving on to a new section.

* * * * *

SELECTING PICTURES

Pictures will significantly enhance the overall appearance of your book. You might like to consider such things as:

- photographs
- certificates
- ration book
- identity card
- sketches
- documents
- school reports
- cartoons

- special cards
- newspaper cuttings.

Achieving the right balance

The majority of pictures are likely to be photographs of family and people who have been significant in your life. Especially with pictures of the family, it is important to ensure a balance. If there are six photos of your daughter and only two of your son, he might feel offended. Counting the number of times that people appear in the book can be revealing.

While you may be besotted with any grandchildren or godchildren, it must be remembered that this is a book about your whole life. The early photographs are usually far more fascinating than those taken relatively recently.

Q: How many photographs should I include?

A: There are no hard and fast rules. Some people have half a dozen pages of pictures, others include 50 or more . . . and four or five pictures can fit on a page. However, the more pages of pictures you include, the greater the reproduction costs.

Photographs are interesting, especially those in your early life, but selecting them is not easy. Ultimately, you can include as many as you like, but remember that this is an autobiography and not a photograph album. The photos should not detract from the writing – they are there to enhance it.

Selecting the right place for the pictures

Placing pictures in a handwritten or typed presentation requires a great deal of forethought and it will be easier to resort to the traditional-style block of pictures, or a page of pictures inserted nearest to the appropriate point.

With a word processor there is far more flexibility and pictures can be placed at the appropriate point in the text.

Adding captions

Captions in a book serve a similar purpose to writing on the backs of photos. While we know who everyone is at the time, with the passing of years it becomes increasingly difficult to identify everyone. Even if the book is aimed at a purely family audience, unless the picture is placed immediately next to the relevant text, it is worth adding captions.

Ensure that the captions are also proofread – any mistakes are likely to be immediately spotted because the pictures will be looked at more often than the text.

Landscape pictures (short and wide like postcards) can be accommodated as easily as portrait style photos (tall and narrow like this book). For landscape pictures, decide which way round they should face and be consistent throughout the book.

Choosing the final picture

The last picture in the book occupies a very significant position. A photograph of yourself in later life is fitting; other favourites are a picture of the whole family, or perhaps one of you and your partner if that is appropriate.

This picture should normally appear on the final page of the book, just before any appendix.

REPRODUCING THE PICTURES

Even for a single book it is unlikely that you will want to use the original photographs or other templates. However, various forms of high quality reproductions can be found at surprisingly affordable prices:

- copy photographs
- photocopying (black and white and colour)
- computer scanning.

Ordering copy photographs

Where you have photographs, copies can be easily ordered from high street or mail order outlets. For other templates take a photograph and then order as many copies as you require.

The pictures can be inserted into the appropriate space left in the text using double-sided tape.

The disadvantage of this process is that the final book will be a little bulky because the photos stand proud of the page.

Using photocopies

While regular black and white copies may be adequate, the quality of colour photocopies is excellent, often being hard to distinguish from the original photograph or document. Copy shops can be found in most high streets.

Photocopying pictures

Pictures up to A4 or even A3 size can be accommodated, being reduced as necessary to fit the size of your book.

If individual copy pictures are to be stuck onto the pages of your manuscript, better value can be obtained by placing several photographs on one page, having them photocopied and then cutting them up.

Once cut to size, the pictures can be inserted with adhesive or double-sided tape at the appropriate place in the text. As photocopies are thinner than photographs, the book will be less bulky than using copy photos.

Photocopying the whole page

An alternative method is to place the photograph within the text and then photocopy the whole page. This can lead to varying results because text and photographs do not always reproduce to the same quality. However, with perseverance, excellent results can be obtained and, of course, the picture remains flush with the page.

A word of warning – if your requirements are too complex or demanding, you may be charged for trial copies as well as the final versions.

Scanning the pictures

Computer technology is such that pictures can be scanned and reproduced in colour to a very high definition; again, it is often difficult to distinguish the reproduction from the original.

Because of the almost limitless flexibility of technology and high quality printers, excellent results can be obtained. The pictures and the text can be manipulated at will, but because of the time-consuming nature of the process, it can be expensive.

REPRODUCING THE TEXT

If your manuscript is handwritten, or typed on a typewriter with no memory, and you only want one copy of the book you can use your original script. However, if, as is likely, several books are required, the manuscript will need to be photocopied.

For those using a word processor and printer, or an electronic typewriter with a memory, this is not an issue as additional copies can be reproduced at the touch of a button.

Pictures scanned into the computer can be printed along with text. If the pictures are to be attached afterwards, an appropriate space will need to be left within the printed page.

Demanding high quality

A good printer is vital for a quality production. Excellent inkjet printers can be purchased for little more than £100, and higher quality laser printers are not much more; alternatively you may be able to borrow one from a friend or grandchild!

Other issues to consider are:

- good quality paper (at least 80 gsm)
- using a new toner cartridge
- leaving plenty of space for pictures.

CONSIDERING AN APPENDIX

An appendix can include anything which does not fit neatly into your story:

- diaries you kept in early life
- the diary or writing of a parent or grandparent
- report cards throughout your school years
- census returns
- a family tree
- a list of important family dates
- songs or poetry
- sketches you performed
- a soapbox
- a log of your round the world cruise.

If you get carried away and the appendix starts to form a life of its own, it might be better to think again. You could perhaps place these materials in a special box in which you keep your book. This will ensure that the appendix does not detract from the intended focus of the book – your life story.

Including reminiscences from the wider family

If you have asked your children, or perhaps a sibling, cousin or friend, to write a few pages, it is likely to fit comfortably as an appendix.

An account written by your partner can be included as an appendix, but it is usually best found within the main body of the book.

Producing a family tree

A family tree that fits onto a single page of your book can be readily accommodated as an appendix. However, family trees have a tendency to extend with the enthusiasm of research. If it cannot be produced on a single page, or perhaps folded into a reasonable size to be slotted into the back of the book, it might be best not to include it.

An advantage of keeping the family tree separate is that it can be updated as the need arises and new copies can replace those that become dog-eared and torn with regular unfolding. It can perhaps be kept in the presentation box along with the book.

How you produce the family tree is up to you. Plenty of computer programs are available, but a well-presented handwritten diagram will convey the same information.

CHECKLIST

- Have you included everyone who has helped you with the book in the acknowledgements?

- Are you happy with the balance of pictures?

- Have you checked for consistency in the text, and the layout of the pages and headings?

ASSIGNMENTS

- Decide on the size of the book and how it is to be presented: hand-written, typed or word processed.

- Finalise the introductory pages.

- Investigate how you would like to reproduce the pictures.

- Produce the final draft of the book.

13

Production

This chapter suggests ways in which you can produce up to several dozen books for friends and family. Other methods of production and wider publishing are considered in the final chapter.

PRODUCING A SINGLE VOLUME

Now that you have the final manuscript of your book, possibly also including pictures, you are in a position to have it transformed into a book.

Whether your manuscript is handwritten, typed or word processed, you have several options available to you.

Having your manuscript bound

Witnessing a pile of paper being transformed into a book is an amazing experience. In the hands of an expert bookbinder, the manuscript is stitched and bound, providing a beautiful and fitting presentation for all your hard work.

Most universities will be happy to recommend the bookbinder they use for PhD theses; alternatively, the telephone directory may list a local firm. Depending on what material is used (leather, buckram, etc.), it is likely to cost in the region of £20 to £30 per copy.

Q: I want to have my book bound – how many pages does it need to be?

A: For a book to be bound you should have at least 75 sheets – 150 sides. Up to 500 sides can be accommodated comfortably before considering dividing your work into a second volume.

If you need to increase the number of pages you have several options:

– write more
– include more pictures
– consider an appendix or two
– encourage other contributions.

With the use of a word processor you can also:

– opt for a book with smaller dimensions
– increase the margins
– increase the font size.

It is likely that you will choose several of the above and play around with different page layouts before you arrive at the presentation that is most pleasing to the eye.

Incorporating larger pictures
With careful folding it should be possible to include the occasional large picture or, more likely, a family tree. The bookbinder is likely to guillotine the edge of the book, so discuss how any special pages should be folded.

If this service cannot be offered, the bookbinder may be willing to add a small pocket in the back or front inside cover in which to hold a folded sheet of paper.

Considering other forms of presentation
More modest productions will include:

● a ring binder
● a photograph album
● spiral binding (plastic or wire)
● heat-treated glue bindings
● metal clamp bindings.

High street copy shops will be able to assist with at least some of the above. Additionally, large office superstores have an abundance of presentation ideas and are worth investigating.

PRODUCING MULTIPLE COPIES

Increasing production
Your master manuscript can be photocopied and produced in the same

manner as the single volume to achieve as many copies of your book as required. The copy shop will tell you what format they require and the associated costs for black and white or colour copies.

You will need to check that the books have been properly collated before having them bound.

Books with colour pictures and a quality binding are likely to cost upwards of £50 each depending on how many pictures are included. If you intend charging for the books, it is worth checking in advance who is prepared to pay, otherwise you may end up with more copies on your hands than you had intended.

Printing your own copies

If you are using a word processor, it may be that additional copies of the book can be produced more reasonably and to a higher standard on your own printer rather than having them photocopied.

If you are producing the pictures on your own printer there will be a trade-off between quality and cost. In both instances it is worth undertaking some research and comparing prices.

Using an external company

If you have a wide circle of friends and require dozens of copies of your book, the above means of production may be too expensive.

The advance of technology makes it possible to produce a modest number of books in a cost-effective manner. This is discussed in the next chapter under the context of self-publishing.

CELEBRATING YOUR BOOK

You have finished – well done!

Whether you have produced one book or several, you have achieved a major feat. So many people say, 'I could write a book,' but very few do so.

Savour the moment and perhaps throw a party for your book launch. If it has been written in secret, you can plan the surprise unveiling of your book. You might even want to invite the local press.

Failing that, why not go out for a special dinner to mark the occasion – after all, it's not every day that you write a book. Don't forget to include those who've helped; they will want to share your special day.

Again, well done.

WHAT NEXT?

With all the time you will find that you now have on your hands, there are any number of possibilities open to you. Perhaps you can consider:

- reading your book onto a tape recorder or video camera
- joining a writing circle
- setting up a life writing class
- writing articles for magazines
- researching your family tree
- helping others with their books
- writing a sequel!

CHECKLIST

- Are you happy with the binding? Having come this far you don't want to spoil the overall presentation for the sake of a few pounds.

- Are you sure about how many copies of the book you require?

ASSIGNMENTS

- Plan your book launch.

- Relax and enjoy the party.

14

Publishing

Publishing is a complex industry and while it is not the main intention of this book to encourage authors in this direction, some ideas and warnings are provided for the more adventurous.

Considering publishing

Various forms of publishing exist, and not all are what they claim to be. Many people have paid significant sums of money for little in return, so tread very carefully. Vanity publishers like to refer to their services as 'self-publishing', so read this whole section carefully.

For ease of discussion, publishing shall be considered under three broad categories:

- mainstream publishing
- self-publishing
- vanity publishing.

UNDERSTANDING MAINSTREAM PUBLISHING

Writing that bestseller

We have all heard of the unknown author writing a best-seller . . . we rarely hear of the tens of thousands who remain unknown.

If you suspect that your manuscript may appeal to a wider audience you might be tempted to look for a publisher.

Identifying mainstream publishers

Mainstream publishers do not expect any payment; they receive their return from a percentage of the sale of the books. Indeed, some publishers even give an advance, but to receive one you are likely to be a nationally known figure, or at least have a track record as an author.

Being realistic, you will not receive an advance, and are extremely unlikely to have your manuscript accepted by a reputable publisher.

Slogging around

Hundreds of publishers and the types of books in which they specialise are listed in *The Artists' and Writers' Yearbook* and *The Writers' Handbook*. Many will not accept unsolicited manuscripts, but others are happy to do so. Research well, be patient and do not raise your hopes.

Publishers usually require a synopsis of the book and a sample chapter. By enclosing a stamped addressed envelope your manuscript should be returned to you.

Finding an agent

You may be very lucky and find an agent who will hawk your manuscript round publishing houses on your behalf. However, finding an agent is likely to be equally as difficult as approaching the publisher in the first place.

Agents are also listed in *The Artists' and Writers' Yearbook* and *The Writers' Handbook*.

WARNING

If you have seen an advert offering to publish your book, in all likelihood this will not be a mainstream publisher as they rarely advertise – they don't need to as they are hounded by dozens of would-be authors every day.

CONSIDERING SELF-PUBLISHING

A more realistic outlet for the unknown autobiographer is via self-publishing. Here the author arranges for a number of books to be printed, registers the ISBN (see page 128) and then undertakes any promotion of the books. Essentially, the author also becomes the publisher.

Some authors are happy with a limited number of copies to give or sell to a largely known audience, perhaps with the option of ordering more copies if demand goes well. Others relish a greater challenge and want to try their chances in appealing to a wider audience.

Understanding the risks

Self-publishing involves the author taking the risk of production in the hope of recouping those costs and, hopefully, more when and if the book is sold. The onus remains with the author to sell the books. This is fine as long as you go in with your eyes open and are prepared to accept the risks.

Books were traditionally ordered from a printer, but with the advance of technology, computer-generated books offer an increasingly attractive option to the author.

Looking for a local printer

If you require at least 500 copies of your book it is worth obtaining a quotation from your local printer. You will be advised as to what is involved and be provided with a fixed price for the books. Armed with this information you can investigate what sort of market there might be for your book.

The price of books from a printer becomes increasingly attractive the more you order. However, don't be tempted to order thousands when you know that you only have requests for 53 copies . . . you may end up with an awful lot of books under your bed.

Considering computer generated books

Books generated by computer incur fewer overheads than a printing press. Set-up costs are lower and so competitive prices can be offered for a modest number of books. These can be ordered in units of twenty or thirty at a time, rather than hundreds as with conventional printing. If the author waits for confirmed orders before requesting a batch of books, the risk is reduced solely to the original set-up cost.

Taking precautions
If you order any books from a third party:

- Ensure that you have a written quotation of all costs before embarking on any venture.
- Ask to see samples of the type of book you will receive.
- Speak to previous customers.
- Ensure that you will receive a proof before the books are printed, and check this proof thoroughly – it is your responsibility.

With the options considered so far you will know how much the books cost in advance. Whoever undertakes the book production makes no guarantees as to how many may be sold – that is entirely up to you.

Beware of anyone who makes claims about how many books you will sell, especially if you are paying for the privilege.

Obtaining an ISBN

Published books require an International Standard Book Number, a unique number that will allow your book to be ordered from anywhere in the world. This is obtained from J. Whitaker and Sons Ltd, the address for which can be found at the back of this book.

While the service is free, you will be required to provide six copies of your book for depositing in various libraries. It also entitles you to an entry in the magazine *Bookseller*, which is received by bookshops.

You will need to nominate a publisher. This is likely to be yourself and you will then be contacted by any bookshop that receives an order for your book. Again, don't raise your hopes; unless your book receives tremendous publicity, you are unlikely to receive many (if any) orders.

Promoting your book

Those who receive a precious copy of your book are likely to be delighted — after all, it has been lovingly written by their friend. Don't be tempted into thinking that such praise means that the book is destined to become a bestseller.

Testing the market

The real measure as to the commercial success of your book is whether people who do not know you are prepared to pay for it. To test this it is worth seeking independent advice, but this should not be sought from anyone who will ultimately charge you money — they are likely to say what you want to hear!

Approaching local bookshops
Local bookshops will be a potential outlet, but valuable shelf space will not be offered unless it is felt that your book will sell.

Before having any books printed, seek the opinion of the managers of these shops, asking such questions as:

- Would there be any demand for such a book?
- If so, in what numbers?
- What should the price of the book be?
- What percentage would the bookshop charge?
- Can you show me any similar books?
- How many copies were sold?

Bookshop managers will also give advice on printers of similar books, and probably also provide contact details of local people who have undertaken similar ventures. It is well worth approaching other such authors for their advice and warnings.

Having the book reviewed
The local newspaper will probably be happy to review your original book. You could mention that you are considering having the book printed and that anyone interested in a copy should contact you. The response you receive will help determine whether to proceed with a wider publishing venture.

Most people interested in buying a copy will be happy to wait a few months while books are being printed.

If your story includes a particular subject, like your time in the RAF, a specialist magazine or service association may be happy to review it.

Placing articles
If a magazine is happy to print a few pages of your book in the form of an article, this will help you gauge its wider appeal. If you are fortunate, you may even be able to persuade the magazine to pay you a few pounds for your efforts.

Asking friends
While friends are likely to speak favourably about your book, if you have wider aspirations it will be worth asking them whether they know of people who would be happy to buy a copy. If the result is a diplomatic, 'They can borrow mine,' then perhaps the market will not be quite as buoyant as you had hoped.

This may sound harsh, but it's better to be disappointed early on rather than to build your hopes, pay out good money and then be disappointed.

Making it work
While the advice here has been to err on the side of caution, some people make a success of self-publishing and have a hugely enjoyable time in the process. Success is usually measured by covering costs rather than making money, but they have the satisfaction of knowing that their book has been read by a wider audience than would otherwise be the case.

UNDERSTANDING VANITY PUBLISHING

Vanity publishers feast upon the unrealistic optimism of new authors. Understandably, they never advertise their services as vanity publishers, being more likely to call themselves 'cooperative publishers', 'subsidy publishers' or even using the generic title of self-publishing.

Vanity publishers imply that huge quantities of your book will be sold, although they are careful not to state this in writing. Rarely do they sell more than one or two copies – that is essentially left to you. No company can guarantee large sales . . . and if they could, they should be offering you an advance in the first place.

Furthermore, you often do not even receive the books until you make sales, in the process sending even more money on top of the substantial prepayment!

If you spend money, at least get books in return and be prepared to sell them yourself.

Consulting an authority

Over the past ten years, Johnathon Clifford has worked tirelessly to raise the public awareness of vanity publishing. He has become a recognised authority and received considerable media coverage. His free advice service is available to all, so if you have any concerns, contact him – details can be found at the end of this book.

CHECKLIST

- Are you sure you want to embark on publishing?

- If you have been asked to pay, are you comfortable with what is being offered? Have you seen samples of the work you are expecting and spoken to past clients?

ASSIGNMENTS

- If you are considering publishing, write a list of people who have confirmed that they would like to buy a copy.

- Research alternative methods of production.

Glossary

Advance. A sum paid to the author in advance of publication of a book.

Agent. See **literary agent**.

Artistic Licence. A term used for the author to embellish the writing, particularly with regard to stretching the truth.

Autobiography. A life story written by the person concerned.

Biography. A life story researched and written by someone other than the subject of the book. The term is also often used generically to refer to both biographies and autobiographies.

Cliffhanger. A writing technique found at the end of a chapter or even a book, designed to keep the reader wanting more.

Copyright. The exclusive right to written, electronic or oral material. The ownership rests with the author unless legally assigned to a third party.

Draft. Any early version of the manuscript.

Edit. To revise a manuscript looking for mistakes, repetitions, ambiguities, inconsistencies and omissions, to improve the work.

Flashback. A writing technique where the story jumps back in time. Useful for dramatic effect, or to help overcome difficulties with the chronology, especially in a book covering the life of more than one person.

House style. A set of guidelines regarding the use of punctuation, numbering systems etc. to ensure consistency throughout a work.

ISBN. International Standard Book Number, a unique ten-digit reference number allocated by J. Whitaker and Sons Ltd to identify and aid the reordering of published books.

Ghostwriter. A third party who writes about the person who is the subject of the book, usually with the subject's assistance, but not necessarily so in the case of an unauthorised biography. Any credit given to the ghostwriter is usually couched in such words as 'with assistance from . . .'

GSM. Grams per square metre – the weight system applied to paper.

Internet. Global computer network with a standard addressing system.

Libel. Writing which damages a person's reputation or livelihood.

Life story. Autobiography or biography.

Literary agent. A person who acts on behalf of the author in dealings with the publisher – both offering the work and negotiating contracts. Usually receiving a commission in the order of 10–15% from what the author receives, the agent is paid by results.

Manuscript. The handwritten, typed or word processed material which represents work in progress prior to a book being produced.

Memoir. An autobiography, usually in the form of selected anecdotes rather than a detailed, chronological life story.

Oral history. Recording the spoken word on tape.

Pagination. The laying out of a page with text and/or pictures in preparation for the final book.

Proofread. To review the manuscript thoroughly, usually just prior to printing, to eliminate mistakes and inconsistencies.

Vanity publishing. A term applied when an author pays to have a book published.

Web page. A private text and graphical 'page' on the Internet.

Useful Addresses

Age Exchange, The Reminiscence Centre, 11 Blackheath Village, London SE3 9LA. Tel: (020) 8318 9105.
Website: *www.age-exchange.org.uk*
BBC Education, Room 3318, White City, London, W12 7TS.
Tel: 08700 100222. Website: *www.bbc.co.uk/education*
Bound Biographies Ltd, Boundary House, 23 Thompson Drive, Bicester, Oxfordshire OX27 8FA. Tel: 01869 321727.
Website: *www.boundbiographies.com*
The British Library National Sound Archive, 29 Exhibition Road, London SW7 2AS. Tel: (020) 7589 6603.
Website: *www.bl.uk./collections/sound-archive*
The British Library Newspaper Library, Colindale Avenue, London NW9 5HE. Tel: (020) 7412 7353.
Website: *www.bl.uk/collections/newspaper*
Johnathan Clifford, 27 Mill Road, Fareham, Hampshire PO16 0TH. Tel: 01329 822218. Website: *http//ourworld.compuserve.com/home-pages/johnathonclifford*
Directory of Writers' Circles, Jill Dick, 'Oldacre', Horderns Park Road, Chapel-en-le-Frith, Derbyshire SK23 9SY. (Please enclose a cheque for £5 payable to Jill Dick.) Tel: 01298 812305.
Website: *www.cix.co.uk/~oldacre*
The Federation of Worker Writers and Community Publishers (FWWCP), 67 The Boulevard, Tunstall, Stoke-on-Trent ST6 6BD. Tel: 01782 822327. Website: *www.fwwcp.mcmail.com*
The Oral History Society, c/o Department of Sociology, Essex University, Colchester, Essex CO4 3SQ. Tel: (020) 7412 7405.
Website: *www.oralhistory.org.uk*
The Overseas Pensioner, 138 High Street, Tonbridge, Kent TN9 1AX. Tel: 01732 363836.

The Royal British Legion, 48 Pall Mall, London SW1Y 5JY.
  Tel: (020) 7973 7200. Website: *www.britishlegion.org.uk*
The Society of Authors, 84 Drayton Gardens, London SW10 9SB.
  Tel: (020) 7373 6642. Website: *www.writers.org.uk/society*
J. Whitaker and Sons Ltd (ISBNs), The Standard Book Numbering
  Agency, 12 Dyott Street, London WC1A 1DF. Tel: (020) 7420 6008.
  Website: *www.whitaker.co.uk/isbn.htm*

OTHER REFERENCE MATERIALS

British Newspaper Library – see above
National Sound Archive – see above
Nostalgia Museums
Videos – *A Year to Remember* series (Telstar Video Entertainment)
The 1940s House (Wall to Wall Television for Channel 4) 2000

TYPING AND PROOFREADING SERVICES

Recommendations can usually be found from the local Writers' Circle,
library or typing college. Advertisements can also be found in the
magazine Writer's News and in the Yellow Pages.

Further Reading

BOOKS

Brief Guide to Self-Publishing, Ann Kritzinger (£2.50 post paid from Book-in-Hand, 20 Shepherds Hill, London N6 5AH).
Chronicle of the 20th Century, Dorling Kindersley.
Creative Writing, Adèle Ramet, How to Books.
Starting to Write, Marina and Deborah Oliver, How To Books.
The 1940s House, Juliet Gardiner, Channel 4 Books.
The Writer's Handbook, Macmillan.
Writers' and Artists' Yearbook, A. & C. Black.
Writing for Publication, Chriss McCallum, How To Books.

MAGAZINES

Best of British, Ian Beacham Publishing, Bank Chambers, 27a Market Deeping, Lincolnshire PE6 8EA. Tel: 01778 342814.
Website: *www.best-of-british.com*
Evergreen, PO BOX 52, Cheltenham, Gloucestershire GL50 1YQ. Tel: 01242 537900. Website: *www.thisengland.co.uk*
Goodtimes, Jeffreys Place, Camden, London NW1 9PP. Tel: 020 7428 3000. Website: *www.arp.org.uk*
The Overseas Pensioner, 138 High Street, Tonbridge, Kent TN9 1AX. Tel: 01732 363836.
Saga, Saga Publishing Ltd, The Saga Building, Middelburg Square, Folkestone, Kent CT20 1AZ. Tel: 01303 771111.
Website: *www.saga.co.uk/publishing*
Writers' News and *Writing Magazine*, PO Box 168, Wellington Street, Leeds, W. Yorkshire LS17 8NT. Tel: (0113) 238 8333.
Website: *www.writersnews.co.uk*
Yours, Apex House, Oundle Road, Peterborough, PE2 9NP. Tel: 01733 898100.

Index

WRITING FOR PUBLICATION
How to sell your work and succeed as a writer

Chriss McCallum

Absorbing and highly informative, this is the fourth edition of Chriss McCallum's essential handbook. No author seriously interested in getting published can afford to be without it. 'Handy for both professionals and new-comers alike.' *Writers' News*. 'Really definitive. . . leaves every other similar book in its shade.' *Pause*. 'As valuable as the highway code is to the motorist.' *Steve Wetton's* Introduction. 'I wholeheartedly recommend this book.' *QWF*.

192pp. illus. 1 85703 226 8. 4th edition.

AWAKEN THE WRITER WITHIN
How to discover and release your true writer's voice

Cathy Birch

'takes you on a journey into the subconscious to help you find that voice – and use it. The results can be both amazing and satisfying.' *Writers' Own*. 'There is a solid, practical base to Cathy's book. . . Give Cathy's methods a try, you might surprise yourself.' *Writers' Bulletin*.

144pp. 1 85703 656 5. 2nd edition.

THE WRITER'S GUIDE TO RESEARCH
An invaluable guide to gathering material for features, novels and non-fiction books

Marion Field

Whether you are writing fact or fiction, good research is essential if you want to add authority and vitality to your work. This valuable resource book gives thorough help on conducting effective research, shows how to find the material you need, and how to use it. Find out how to save time *and* improve the quality of your information. Marion Field is an experienced freelance writer and has published both articles and biographies. She is the author of several reference books for writing including *Improving Your Written English*.

104pp. illus. 1 85703 574 7.

WRITE & SELL YOUR NOVEL
The fiction writer's guide to writing for publication

Marina Oliver

If you want to write a novel, the second edition of this popular handbook is the guide you need. Step by step it shows you how to get started, how to create compelling characters, plots and subplots, and whose viewpoint to tell your story from. There are tips on how to prepare your work for submission, who to send it to and an overview of the whole publishing process. Don't start writing without it! Marina Oliver has published over 30 novels, historical and contemporary, and lectures widely on writing.

144pp. illus. 1 85703 575 5. 2nd edition.

WRITER'S GUIDE TO COPYRIGHT AND LAW
Get your full financial reward and steer clear of legal pitfalls

Helen Shay

Now updated for its second edition, this invaluable guide covers all aspects of .
copyright and law which affect writers and writing, including advances, agents,
contracts, copyright, ideas kidnapping, libel, literary estate, rights, royalties and
self-publishing as well as potential danger zones and the best safeguards. 'Vital
information for every writer.' *Writer's Book Society*. 'Very informative and
useful – I wish our legal editors could manage to put their books into such
plain language.' *Barnes & Taylor Solicitors*. Helen Shay is a solicitor of over
15 years standing, who has also tutored in business law and was formerly a
legal columnist for *Writing Magazine*.

96pp. illus. 1 85703 551 8. 2nd edition.

CREATIVE WRITING
How to develop your writing skills for successful fiction and non-fiction
work

Adèle Ramet

Now in its fourth edition, this useful book guides you through key techniques,
with exercises aimed at helping you to write more effectively in your chosen
genre. You'll see how to approach your work from different angles, how to
bring a fresh slant to non-fiction pieces, how to build characters, setting and
dialogue in your fiction. Whatever your writing interest, this book will help
you write more creatively and lead you further along the route towards publication. 'This is a book which merits a place on every writer's bookshelf.' *Writer's
Bulletin*.

136pp. illus. 1 85703 852 5. 4th edition.

WRITING A CHILDREN'S BOOK
How to write for children <u>and</u> get published

Pamela Cleaver

Do you dream of seeing your children's book on shelves in bookshops and libraries? This exciting book gives thorough, practical guidance to help turn your dreams into reality. Discover how to create gripping plots and memorable characters. Look at the whole range of options available to children's writers – including picture books, series books, and books for young adults. There's also advice on editing techniques and information on how to approach publishers. Written by a successful children's author, editor and creative writing tutor, this book is a must for aspiring children's writers.

144pp. illus. 1 85703 598 4.

WRITE & SELL YOUR NOVEL
The fiction writer's guide to writing for publication

Marina Oliver

If you want to write a novel, the second edition of this popular handbook is the guide you need. Step by step it shows you how to get started, how to create compelling characters, plots and subplots, and whose viewpoint to tell your story from. There are tips on how to prepare your work for submission, who to send it to and an overview of the whole publishing process. Don't start writing without it! Marina Oliver has published over 30 novels, historical and contemporary, and lectures widely on writing.

144pp. illus. 1 85703 575 5. 2nd edition.

CREATIVE WRITING
How to develop your writing skills for successful fiction and non-fiction work

Adèle Ramet

Now in its third edition, this useful book guides you through key techniques, with exercises aimed at helping you to write more effectively in your chosen genre. You'll see how to approach your work from different angles, how to bring a fresh slant to non-fiction pieces, how to build characters, setting and dialogue in your fiction. Whatever your writing interest, this book will help you write more creatively and lead you further along the route towards publication. 'This is a book which merits a place on every writer's bookshelf.' *Writer's Bulletin.*

136pp. illus. 1 85703 699 9. 3rd edition.